Blending Families

Blending Families

Merging Households with Kids 8–18

Trevor Crow Mullineaux
and Maryann Karinch

ROWMAN & LITTLEFIELD
Lanham • Boulder • New York • London

Published by Rowman & Littlefield
A wholly owned subsidiary of The Rowman & Littlefield Publishing Group, Inc.
4501 Forbes Boulevard, Suite 200, Lanham, Maryland 20706
www.rowman.com

Unit A, Whitacre Mews, 26-34 Stannary Street, London SE11 4AB, United Kingdom

British Library Cataloguing in Publication Information Available

Library of Congress Cataloging-in-Publication Data

The hardback edition of this book was previously cataloged by the Library of Congress
as follows:

Names: Crow Mullineaux, Trevor, author. | Karinch, Maryann, author.
Title: Blending families : merging households with kids 8-18 / by Trevor Crow
    Mullineaux and Maryann Karinch.
Description: Lanham : Rowman & Littlefield, 2016. | Includes bibliographical references
    and index.
Identifiers: LCCN 2015041627 | ISBN 9781442243101 (cloth : alk. paper) | ISBN
    9781442243118 (electronic) | ISBN 9780810895683 (paper : alk. paper)
Subjects: LCSH: Stepfamilies.
Classification: LCC HQ759.92.C76 2016 | DDC 306.874/7—dc23
LC record available at http://lccn.loc.gov/2015041627

♾™ The paper used in this publication meets the minimum requirements of
American National Standard for Information Sciences—Permanence of Paper
for Printed Library Materials, ANSI/NISO Z39.48-1992.

Printed in the United States of America

Disclaimer

The cases described in this book are based on incidents. However, except when otherwise specified, names and specific details have been changed at the request of interviewees who wish to remain anonymous. Therefore, any likeness that might be found with any living individual, except when specified, is unintended.

Contents

Author's Note

TREVOR TALKS ABOUT HER OWN BLENDED FAMILIES—PAST AND PRESENT

My dad's mother died when he was eleven years old. He was the oldest of four siblings, with the youngest being just two. The family never spoke of it. They were an Irish Catholic brood back in the 1940s when more young mothers than today were dying in childbirth or "female" diseases. When they left young ones behind, the drill was for the father to find a new mother for his children.

My father, his brother, and two sisters were told to go across the street and stay for a few days. The funeral happened, and after that, they went back home and were told never to speak of it again.

My grandfather remarried, thinking that he was giving his children a loving woman to care for them. She turned out to be mean-spirited.

On his deathbed, my father said that one of the worst things about growing up involved Frank, his step-brother. My father's stepmother made sure that Frank got his orange juice and a newspaper delivered to his room every morning. For everyone else, the rules were different—all day long.

As an aftermath to this already bad story, Frank ran off with my Uncle Tommy's first wife and she took the kids; in other words, he ran off with his step-brother's wife and two children.

This didn't taint my view of blended families, because I didn't even know how awful my father's life was until after I had a blended family of my own.

I had a few years of the single life after earning my MBA, and then met and married a divorced man with two young children. Abruptly, I went from a self-focused *Sex and the City* life to an other-focused world of *Instant Mom*. It also didn't take long until I was both a stepmom and a biological mom. It was at that point I realized something important for every parent who undertakes blending families: As rich, intimate, and wonderful as the bond between a stepparent and child can be, it differs in fundamental "animal" ways from the relationship with biological children. We can *decide* to care for, and may even come to love, another person's children, but nature gives us a relationship with our biological children that has nothing to do with decisions. I realized this acutely when my first child was an infant. She smelled like flowers to me; it was a lovely, enticing smell. When I held her and I had a stepchild on my lap at the same time, I was struck by the difference in smell between the two of them! Biology gives us certain triggers so that we want to be near our children. This kind of response has clear advantages for any species since the urge for a mother to stay close to her young helps protect against predators.

It occurred to me when I noticed the difference in smell that, since I wasn't experiencing the biological cues telling me to be close to my stepchildren, I had to make a conscious decision to put myself there. I had to develop a level of sensitivity to their needs because it wasn't coming naturally to me.

For a taste of how our family blended—or at least my husband's two children and our two children came together forever—read the short essay that my biological daughter, Olivia, wrote about her half-sister, Michelle. It's inserted at the end of the chapter on preteens and before the one on teens because Olivia is recalling an event that occurred when she was 10 and Michelle was 16. Michelle and her brother Spencer have been a part of my life throughout my biological children's lives. Nonstop. No matter what happened between their father and me. When Olivia turned 16 and she was allowed to take one friend on a special trip, the one friend she chose was Michelle.

In marrying Vinnie when my children were 11 and 13, he and I committed to yet another blending adventure. His twelve-year-old daughter, Eva, had been an only child until she moved in with us during the week because she was attending the same school as my daughter and we lived close to it. She would go back to being an only child on the weekends that she spent with her mother, whose home was a much greater distance from the school. So apart from the usual challenges associated with blending, Eva now had to deal with sharing the spotlight with siblings. She brought a great attitude to the process and made it clear that having a sister and brother was a good thing for her.

We could have had a rocky start, though. The day before Vinnie and I were getting married we faced our first test about how these children of ours would feel about each other and about the fairness of our parenting.

When Eva, accompanied by her BFF, was brought to the hotel where the ceremony would take place, she was told that the only room available was a suite. The front desk checked her and her friend into it. Vinnie and I didn't even have a suite! We knew if we let her stay there, it would cause resentment with her new stepsiblings, so she and her friend moved into our room and Vinnie and I took the suite.

The kids saw that he and I stood together on the decision and that we were being fair to everyone. That simple event helped us set the tone for our joint venture as parents/stepparents.

Now that you know a little of my personal experience of hoop-jumping, holding my ground, and celebrating related to the blending process, I want to take you back a generation to the unions of my divorced parents that led to both wonderful and odd outcomes.

In the years I've been married to Vinnie, and in the years I've been working with Maryann on books about relationships, neither had ever heard me talk about my stepmother until the spring of 2015. I had not even suggested that I had a stepmother. She was simply the woman who married my father when I was already an adult. We had no connection and since she didn't seem to be present physically or emotionally during my father's prolonged, fatal illness, she didn't occupy a spot in my thoughts. In some ways, unrelated to my father, she turned out to be rather courageous. I still never thought of her as part of my family, though.

The "step" that Vinnie and Maryann have heard a lot about is Howard Stevenson, the man my mother married when I was in my mid-20s. My mom brought four young adult women into the family and Howard brought three sons, the youngest of whom was 14 when the families blended. Both my mom and Howard have shown fairness and caring with all seven children in many ways, from time and attention to material resources. Howard even wrote the Foreword for my first book, *Forging Healthy Connections*. He is a professor emeritus at Harvard University, the author of *Getting to Giving: Fundraising the Entrepreneurial Way*, and well known for his work in entrepreneurship—and he openly credits my mom, his wife of more than 25 years now, as being the partner who made much of his success possible. Here's the simple lesson of how my mother and Howard created a blended family: They put each other first and respected each other's children.

Their method of blending has influenced me profoundly. They have had clarity in their intentions regarding each other and all seven children in the family. Naturally, we've had disagreements and temporary rifts, but we share a value system that keeps us coming back to each other as a family.

In this book, we acknowledge that there's a process associated with implementing the basic success formula of "couple first and respect for everyone." We just want to give you enough insight so that the process makes sense in the context of your relationship, and that you have enough tips and "tricks" to handle it so that your family is truly and happily *blended*. The guidance we provide takes the form of both "Do" and "Do Not" so that you can start to build durable attachments from the moment you and your partner decide to join together, and parent together, as a couple.

Introduction

Who Needs This Book?

You choose to become a stepparent. Becoming a biological parent sometimes does not involve planning, and you can never really know what your children will be like. On the other hand, stepparenting reflects a conscious decision to form a family with children whose personalities you didn't help shape when they were little. They are children who don't have your genes; there is a lot you don't know about them physically, emotionally, and psychologically. In so many ways, they are strangers. Despite the challenges, you've decided to be willing to drop certain things that you wanted to do or had intended to do to help out these children who are not yours.

Biological parenting brings different kinds of challenges such as setting expectations based on genes—"I hope he's a good ball player like his dad!"—and trying to do everything right from conception through birth and throughout childhood.

Blending biology, and the requirement to parent, with adult love that fuels the choice to parent involves some unique challenges. We hope to help you meet them.

We have primarily designed this book for couples who are brand new to blending. But we've also given thought to, and included the insights of, people who are contemplating the merger of two families or who have encountered difficulties in the process.

With the baby boomers came myriad opportunities to learn about parenting. Parents, grandparents, and Dr. Spock didn't disappear, but they had plenty of company, like author/experts and family counselors. From T. Berry Brazelton's *Touchpoints* to Haim Ginott's *Between Parent and Child*, the shelves began to fill with parenting advice—and there was just as much marriage advice. Yet for all the resources available on parenting, we didn't see much literature devoted to the distinct challenges of choosing to parent someone else's children.

The book is divided into three parts, with Part I spotlighting the world of challenges you face in blending families. Part II presents what we see as the five critical elements in a successful blend. Part III zeroes in on real stories and practical insights into effecting a blend.

We begin with a guide that helps you understand your own attachment style in the context of your relationship with your partner, and how that style affects the process of blending. Building on your familiarity with attachment styles, the next chapter helps you identify the style that seems to dominate your parenting. We also ask you to turn the tables and try to figure out how your children and stepchildren see your parenting styles. In Chapter 3, we focus on what we think are the five biggest challenges to the blending process—and they start with the importance of putting the couple first. Chapters 4 and 5 explore the issues that a parent or stepparent would confront with preteens and teens, respectively. We emphasize the special challenges that a stepparent faces with kids in these age groups—these kids have a growing need for autonomy, but still need a close and regular connection to parental support and caring.

The second section of the book is devoted to understanding and meeting core emotional needs within a blended family. Trust, vulnerability, empathy, and truth are not fuzzy concepts and "nice to haves." They are *must haves* and they embody concrete realities about how people forge sustainable, healthy relationships. These elements will help you to cocreate the "two Bs" with your partner: belonging and belief. Every person in your family needs to feel like someone who belongs and is loved. Everyone also has to believe that you are in the adventure of blending together. The final chapter in this section is about structure, which involves things like boundaries and routines. The secret to blending is not merely having them in place; it's having them take shape in a way that reflects trust, vulnerability, empathy, and truth. You need the emotional underpinnings that give structure meaning in the context of your family.

The third section is real stories from real people. They don't all have happy Hollywood endings, but even the families that continue to struggle have a great deal to teach all of us about how to create a successful blend. We also consolidate the advice we heard from people who have done a good job of blending, although we didn't take the advice at face value. We look at it through the lens of attachment and by incorporating complementary insights from some of the most respected experts in fields such as family counseling, psychology, and sociology.

The information and stories in the book came together with the help of many, many families who contributed their stories to us personally, participated in surveys, and posted comments and insights in blogs and through social media. These families reflect the many ways that modern families can come together and evolve: marriage and remarriage involving a man and a woman, gay marriages, and the inclusion of a newly transgender parent or gay stepparent. All forms of blended families face the same basic issues and have the same opportunities for emotional bonding.

We also benefited greatly from the scientific research of people who had awe-inspiring curiosity about why human relationships benefit so much when the people involved feel trustworthy, vulnerable, empathetic, and truthful with each other. Most importantly, they also teach us a great deal about how to develop them within our relationships.

As you begin reading, we ask you to shove aside those grim statistics about success rates of second and third and fourth marriages. We want you to say out loud: "The odds are now in my favor."

Part I

OPPORTUNITIES AND CHALLENGES

Blending is a grand experiment. Your family is unique, with each member having special capabilities and quirks and, of course, likes and dislikes. A prime unifying factor that human beings have is yearning to be loved. That includes being seen and heard by people close to them, who also make sure they feel safe to be themselves. Every person wants a sense of belonging, purpose, and acceptance.

The United States Census Bureau describes a blended family this way:

Blended families are formed when remarriages occur or when children living in a household share only one or no biological parents. The presence of a stepparent, stepsibling, or half sibling designates a family as blended.[1]

Your blend is a challenge and an opportunity. The challenge is uniting all those quirks and possible dislikes into a unit—your distinctive version of a family. The opportunity is having that unit evolve into a group of loving people who care for each other and give each other comfort in hard times and celebration in up times. "Family" can imply a biological connection, but today, it does only about half the time. The 2009 census of the United States Census Bureau indicates that 5.6 million children lived with at least one step-parent, about 50 percent of US families involve remarriages or re-coupling, and an average of 1,300 new stepfamilies form every day.[2] So more than ever, family can be composed of people who love and show up for one another with or without biological ties.

This first section of the book introduces a concept that is important throughout each chapter: attachment styles. It's a term that many therapists use to describe the nature of emotional bonding between people, that is, how people connect with others—mainly, how children and parents connect with each other and how people in an intimate relationship connect. Knowing your attachment style as a partner and parent gives you the foundation for making the best use of the insights contained in the later chapters.

As you walk this bumpy, imperfect path to blending, you may find joy, love, and connection, but you are also likely to find plenty of frustration, hurt and, at times, anger. Your substantial opportunity is to grow something greater than any one person—to create an environment where each individual can thrive, feel safe, and give back to the world.

Love greatly, listen openly, and show up for one another as much as possible.

NOTES

1. Rose M. Kreider and Renee Ellis, "Living Arrangements of Children: 2009"; Household Economic Studies, United States Census Bureau; report issued June 2011, p. 1; https://www.census.gov/prod/2011pubs/p70-126.pdf.

2. Ibid.

Chapter 1

The Practical Meaning of Attachment Styles

In 1969, television audiences met *The Brady Bunch*, a newly blended family. Mom brought three girls to the mix and dad brought three boys. We knew that Mike Brady was a widower, but Carol's marital history remained a mystery, as did the circumstances of their meeting, when and how the kids met each other, and any other detail that could have suggested the new couple had "baggage." The only hint we get that Carol's life had bumps comes just before her wedding to Mike when she tells him, "A few years ago, I thought it was the end of the world."

In 2009, nearly forty years to the day after *The Brady Bunch* began solving family issues with a spoonful of sugar, we meet Jay Pritchett, the patriarch in *Modern Family*, a television show aimed at reflecting family arrangements common today. The family in the television show includes a negligent ex, a helicopter mom, and a gay couple with an adopted daughter. There are no lines like the one Carol Brady lilted to her eight-year-old daughter the day of the wedding: "Cindy, why don't you take Bobby upstairs and tell the girls their new brothers are here."

But did Mike and Carol Brady make all the right moves? Mostly. In the very first episode they made a choice that suggests a classic mistake made by blended families: They felt guilty about spending time alone and ended up taking all the kids on their honeymoon (as well as the dog, cat, and housekeeper). In the sitcom, this "familymoon" was actually a good thing to do, but for many couples, the choice to let child-related guilt guide couple-related choices is often the sign of trouble in the marriage. *The couple is the most important system in a blended family*. The two people need to put each other first.

In clinical terms, *The Brady Bunch* features a couple with secure attachments, whereas *Modern Family* also includes couples who might be characterized as pursuers, withdrawers, and disorganized in terms of their attachment

3

styles. That's probably why most people can relate to the cast of characters surrounding Jay Pritchett more than they can relate to Carol and Mike Brady.

Even people in strong, loving relationships sometimes react to an expression of anger or distress with a comment that minimizes the importance of the emotion, for example. Sometimes they use sarcasm to hide real hurt. Other times, they jump to conclusions about what their partner really means and hunker down in a defensive posture, or lash out.

In the following section, we offer you a short questionnaire to get a sense of your attachment style and, as a corollary, your level of reactivity about certain marital situations and issues. Regardless of what you find out through the questionnaire, give yourself a break. Almost no one but Carol and Mike Brady will come out with a "perfect" score.

WHAT'S YOUR ATTACHMENT STYLE?

Knowing the basics of attachment theory will help you figure out why one partner might pursue, fight, and even bully a spouse; why he or she might get up and leave the room if a discussion gets uncomfortable; or why your partner seems to be fairly consistent with nurturing behaviors and has a lot of patience with you. Your awareness of attachment styles also lays the foundation for understanding your parenting style and that of your partner—the subject of Chapter 2.

For decades, the discussion of attachment in studies and journals centered on human babies, monkey babies, and baboon babies. In the 1980s, the conversation expanded to include attachment in relation to adults, eventually connecting the idea of attachment to romantic love.

Attachment styles, or emotional bonds, develop from birth to two years, and the nature of them depends on the primary caregiver's response to the baby's physical and emotional needs. If the caregiver is secure, emotionally available and able to care for the child, then that engenders a feeling of safety and feeling loved; it leads to secure attachment. An anxious or fearful caregiver makes the baby feel unsafe; the child might become anxious and needy or perhaps the reverse, that is, avoidant. If the caregiver is emotionally or physically unavailable, perhaps addicted to a substance, then the child doesn't feel loved or worthy of love. The result of that early experience could be a chaotic, avoidant, or anxious attachment style.

Adult attachment styles in adulthood are the same as those in childhood, but they are typically assigned different names. The child who turns away from attachment would be the adult who is dismissive or avoidant, that is, a withdrawer. The child who is ambivalent about attachment is the adult who has a chaotic attachment style and tends to be disorganized in relationships.

The secure kid is the autonomous adult—someone who has the ability to regulate himself alone or with the attachment figure. The fearful child is the anxious adult who might be called a pursuer within a relationship.

Many of us would not be categorized as "secure" in our attachments throughout our lives. Estimates from studies with large community samples indicate that 60–65 percent of children are securely attached[1]; however, attachment styles can change. Children might be securely attached until something traumatic such as death, divorce, or illness robs them of their primary attachment figure.

Attachments can also go from insecure to secure. Perhaps you grew up doubtful of whether you were loved, or maybe you ran into your room whenever the slightest bit of conflict arose in the family. Later on, you married someone who consistently gives you a sense of belonging. You feel acknowledged, valued, and safe. This person makes you a priority. All of these factors can move you to a secure attachment.

We learn as we go and, hopefully, become more secure as we mature emotionally. When William and Nan got married, her family and friends said, "This marriage won't last six months." The source of their skepticism was William's upbringing as the only child of parents who were well-off financially. He was coddled by his mother, and loved conditionally by both his parents. In other words, as long as he achieved great things academically and professionally, he was worth loving. On the other hand, Nan came from a large family, but was raised by her mother who was widowed when her oldest child was 12. It was a happy, loving family that pooled resources and worked hard to make ends meet. All five kids eventually made it through college. Nan was secure; William was an anxious pursuer. Over time, it was clear to everyone who knew them that William had left his fears behind, trusted in his marriage, and became what therapists would call "secure." The marriage that was said to be doomed to failure after six months lasted 65 years and three months—up to the day when he passed away at age 95.

Determining Your Attachment Style

The following informal questionnaire will help you determine key things about your attachment style. It's not a test instrument, but just a set of questions to help you understand a little better how you behave and react to your partner and children as well as others in your life. Ideally, the questions will also improve your understanding of why your partner responds to you in a particular way.

1. When your partner expresses frustration or even anger with you, what do you do?

  a. Ask what is going on rather than respond directly to the anger. Your first impulse is to offer help by empathizing with whatever he or she is experiencing.
  b. Pull away. You are afraid that anything you say or do will make matters worse.
  c. Respond directly to the anger and fight back.
  d. Initially pull back, and then turn around and become angry.

2. When your partner brings up a difficult subject that involves some friction between the two of you, how do you respond?
  a. You are open to talking about it.
  b. You try to change the subject or perhaps even leave the room because you "suddenly remembered something you have to do."
  c. You feel as though you're on the defensive; you have an emotional reaction.
  d. You feel unworthy—"I'll never get this right"—and then go on the defensive and respond with anger and blame.

3. When you sense your partner is distant and not interested in your feelings or needs, what do you do?
  a. Ask your partner for attention and understanding; you are open about feeling somewhat isolated and disconnected from that person at the moment.
  b. Close up, with the hope that your partner will pull your thoughts and feelings out of you. You've already decided he or she should know what's going on with you and wonder why you should have to say anything.
  c. Raise your voice and criticize to get attention.
  d. Insist your partner will never understand you—a feeling of hopelessness—and then move to "no one will understand me," which triggers deep anger. You may cycle between sadness and anger.

4. When you disagree, who yells the loudest or says the most?
  a. You tend to listen rather than yell.
  b. You leave the room when your partner starts to yell.
  c. You yell louder than your partner.
  d. You might yell like crazy, but feel you'll never be heard; you give up and withdraw emotionally. You are inconsolable.

5. Who is the first to initiate reconciliation after you have a fight?
  a. It's almost always you.
  b. Your partner tends to be the one.
  c. Sometimes you, sometimes your partner.
  d. You look to reconcile right away, but the moment the partner agrees, you are back off to the races again and resume the fight; you can't cope with someone showing you connection even though you initiated the first repair.

6. When you observe your partner talking to an attractive person of your sex at a party, what do you do?
    a. Wait until later, after the conversation with that person is over, and tell your partner that you had a hard time watching him or her talking to an attractive person. Ask your partner to reassure you because the encounter made you feel worried and vulnerable.
    b. Head straight to the bar, vowing not to talk about it but secretly hoping your partner notices how hurt you are.
    c. Get hot-headed, either interrupting the conversation on the spot or criticizing your partner later, blaming your partner for being insensitive.
    d. React with a huge amount of anger and there is no consoling you; you feel no one could ever love you and that here was another illustration of that belief. You also believe that the other person is probably far more lovable than you.
7. If your partner is visibly upset and asks to talk with you, what do you do?
    a. Both show and say that you will talk. Perhaps you'll sit down to demonstrate that you are committed to the conversation.
    b. Show your reluctance to talk about something when the partner is upset. Even though you might say, "Sure," you are slowly moving toward the door.
    c. Assume that being upset has something to do with you and respond emotionally, either defensively or offensively.
    d. You can't deal with another person's feeling of being upset; it just triggers you to be more upset. You create another drama to pull the attention toward yourself and your dilemma.
8. When your partner experiences an intense negative emotion, such as fear, what do you do?
    a. Reach out in empathy, allowing your partner to feel the intensity of the emotion. You stay with him or her in the experience with the hope of providing comfort and support.
    b. Try to help him or her by using dismissive language like "it's not a big deal," "lots of people feel that way" or "just ignore it."
    c. Try to solve the problem in order to alleviate the emotion or perhaps replace it with a different kind of response; you might try to distract your partner with a story.
    d. You demonstrate that you have more of a right to be fearful; you have difficulty attending to another person's fear or pain and just want the attention to be on you.
9. When an event or conversation heads down the wrong path, what do you do?
    a. Try to get your perspectives in synch so that you have a shared understanding of what happened.

b. Take the blame for the problem yourself, or do some blame-sharing to avoid a disagreement.

c. Blame your partner.

d. Head further down the path and blow it up—you make the situation even worse. When the conversation becomes crazy, you are in your element.

10. If your partner says or does something at a social event that you think is rude or thoughtless, what do you do?

a. Wait for a private moment later and bring it up in a nonjudgmental way.

b. Try to disappear from the scene so no one associates you with the embarrassment, and don't mention the incident to your partner.

c. Jump in with sarcasm that throws the spotlight on your partner's indiscretion and in a way that perhaps makes you look (temporarily) clever.

d. You might try to protect him/her and draw the spotlight to yourself, or you might do something even more outrageous in a weird attempt to take the heat off your partner. The response is over-the-top and/or inappropriate.

Secure

If your common response was "a," then you are probably a securely attached person. As a securely attached adult, you feel worthy of love, whole, and safe to connect emotionally with your partner. For the most part, you are comfortable with your emotions and don't see many barriers to expressing them to your partner. You also have a capacity for empathy and make yourself available for your partner in times of stress, even when he or she seems to be "taking it out on you" just because you're the one in the same room. You're a good listener with your partner and, rather than jump to conclusions with that person, you reserve judgment. One result of your behavior is that you engender trust. You make your partner feel safe with you and appreciated by you. Through actions and words, your partner feels like he or she takes precedence in your life. That does not negate your love for your kids and for your career; it means simply that he or she is clearly a priority.

The adult with secure attachment knows how to balance autonomy needs with relationship needs. This is not to say that "secure" equates to "perfect" in a relationship! Securely attached people can also have unresolved issues.

Withdrawer (Avoidant)

If your dominant choice was the second answer, it's likely you are avoidantly attached—a withdrawer—and tend to dismiss your own emotions.

Emotionally avoidant adults are often fearful of emotional connection; they intrinsically feel unsafe. Perhaps you can't even identify your feelings much of the time. You have a tendency to withdraw when stressed or emotional about something, even going to the point of walking out of the room or the home when your partner gets upset. It's relatively easy for you to feel overwhelmed by another's emotion, and difficult for you to empathize with the anxiety or emotional pain that your partner is feeling.

In relationships, you tend to suppress your emotions and keep other people's emotions at arm's length. They might even think you are cold and sometimes feel abandoned by you emotionally. Confronted with this kind of avoidance of intimacy, some people will lash out in criticism because they think you just don't care. They want to get some kind of emotional connection with you and it isn't happening.

Avoidantly attached people are fearful of rejection, withdrawing from intense emotional displays as a way to survive. This is a sympathetic nervous system response, that is, a fight-flight-or-freeze response that happens without thinking. In this case, the response is flight. Such people aren't weighing the pros and cons of intimacy at the moment and deciding how to behave; the behavior emanates from emotion automatically. They get flooded by another person's intensity and so they shut down. Two avoidantly attached people are like roommates living together, politely sharing space and detached from one another.

Pursuer (Anxious)

If you picked the third answer more often than the others in the questionnaire, you may be a pursuer, that is, an anxiously attached person. Anxious pursuers often have underlying feelings of being unsafe in emotional connection, often feeling unworthy of love and not "whole." As such, you fear your partner will abandon you. You can't let yourself be vulnerable with that person because you don't trust that your partner is consistently there for you. As a result, even when your partner reaches out to you, you may not be able to make the connection.

Pursuers often come across as controlling or jealous, because they believe the way to feel calm and stable is to know where their partner is all the time. This isn't about connection; it is about anxiously attached people trying to feel safe and attempting to calm their sympathetic nervous system.

As we mentioned above, there are three ways to respond to a threat when the sympathetic nervous system kicks in: fight, flight, or freeze. If you are an anxious pursuer, you automatically react to threats by fighting. You might raise your voice, criticize, and blame to try to get attention. The response might be amplified if you have a withdrawing partner who doesn't give you a sufficient amount of the attention you crave. Ironically, your behavior likely has the effect of pushing your withdrawer/avoidant partner even farther away, accomplishing the very opposite of the connection you yearn for.

Two anxious pursuers rarely end up together in the long run; the relationship would be volatile. Both have a great deal of difficulty "co-regulating," that is, reciprocally experiencing a calming effect by connecting with another person. Since they can't calm each another down, the relationship eventually blows up. It might be like how Gloria in *Modern Family* describes the relationship with her ex-husband: "We fight; we make love. We fight; we make love. We fight; we make love." The end was not "make love," of course. It was divorce.

As a couple, an avoidant person and an anxiously attached person generate a negative cycle of behaviors known as pursue-withdraw. This is the most common couple connection; most couples have some elements of pursue-withdraw in their behavior patterns.

Disorganized (Chaotic)

If you responded often or always with the "d" answer, that suggests a disorganized attachment style. A disorganized attachment style stems from feelings of being unworthy of love, unsafe, and broken. Think back to your early life. Did you suffer any trauma? Trauma may not be just a single incident, such as your parents' divorce or a car accident. Trauma could be day-to-day bullying by a sibling, or years of struggle in school because of an undiagnosed learning challenge. If you didn't feel loved and supported in the midst of going through something upsetting, then it is possible that you developed a disorganized attachment style. Typically, you are either very reactive, or very shut down—sometimes reaching out, sometimes withdrawing, sometimes lashing out, sometimes overwhelmed by sadness or numbed out. Your partner may try to "repair" a situation or stop the cycle of anger/helplessness, but you can't seem to let that happen completely. This is one reason why you and your partner would benefit greatly by experiencing therapy that is centered on attachment theory, specifically Emotionally Focused Therapy (EFT). EFT therapists help couples identify emotions and emotional triggers and use that understanding to move toward a more secure relationship.

Disorganized people are like toddlers inside: For the most part, they aren't emotionally evolved enough to feel other people's pain, and wonder why all the attention and/or drama aren't focused on *them*. Because they can't attend to another person's emotions, they relate to the expression of emotion by thinking about how they feel and how the circumstances relate to their needs. People with antisocial personality disorders—people we commonly call psychopaths or sociopaths—are disorganized in their attachments. They are on the extreme end of the spectrum, of course. This designation might describe about one in every 25 people–this statistic is probably on the high side.[2]

Trevor has a client who was headed to her sister's large, formal wedding in Miami. She hoped that their mother wouldn't attend (although her mother did plan on attending), because she knew there would be some drama that the mother would initiate. She knew that her mother could not bear having anyone else be the center of attention. During a session, she told Trevor, "My mother will do something!" If she'd laid money on that prediction, she would have won the bet. This is just like the episode in Season 1 of *Modern Family* called "The Incident," in which there is a flashback to Jay's and Gloria's wedding reception where Jay's former wife—clearly a disorganized individual—makes a raunchy, drunken toast. She focuses on her pain, on how she was "wronged," because she can't stand to see her ex and his new wife experience happiness.

From a writer's perspective, disorganized people embody buckets of outrageous scenarios and hilarious material. From a partner's or a child's perspective, they have the capacity to make daily life chaotic and painful.

If you think you're disorganized, don't give up. The relationship between disorganized Holly Golightly (Audrey Hepburn) and steady-as-a-rock Paul Varjak (George Peppard) ultimately worked in the classic movie *Breakfast at Tiffany's*.

One of the couples that Trevor counseled simply worked the chaos into their marriage. In a rare moment of clarity about herself, the woman said that she felt unlovable and she knew how hard that was on her marriage. The husband turned to her and said, "But I love your crazy!" At a time like that, all a therapist can think is, "Who am I to judge?" Sometimes the reason we love one another is a mystery!

It is very important to know that there is no judgment associated with your answers. Even securely attached people typically have some issues that a therapist might label "unresolved."

In considering your attachment style, there is another key concept to understanding why you may struggle with relationships. You may think it sounds extreme and doesn't apply to you, but it might, and just knowing about this creates opportunities for your emotional growth. The concept is "privation."

In the broadest sense, privation refers to a lack of something, like food or water. In a psychological sense, it refers to a lack of attachment. In the extreme, primary caregivers—parents, siblings, a nanny, or someone else—failed to teach the child how to regulate and co-regulate. But it doesn't necessarily relate to extreme circumstances, which is why Paul Aiken, one of Trevor's colleagues who has written a great deal about privation, notes, "It is part of all of us in varying degrees."[3]

In practical terms, privated individuals lack compassion for themselves and for others and, therefore, don't naturally connect with others in an intimate relationship, whether that is with a partner or with their own children.

Like Trevor, Paul Aiken practices EFT. His writings on privation include ways to help privated individuals through something he calls the "creation of experience."[4] He begins by differentiating between "deprivation" and "privation."

The deprived individual knows something is missing. Maybe he knew a mother's love for the first three years of his life and then his mother died suddenly. He is deprived of her love. In contrast, the privated person doesn't even know what's missing. Sticking to the example of a mother's love, we would say that he never experienced that love in the first place so he has no idea what it feels like.

We encountered a version of privation during our interviews for this book. Mark had a half-sister named Mary Ellen who was twenty years older than he was. She was in college in Washington, DC, 700 miles away from the family home in Maine, and had graduated by the time he recognized her as his sister. He wasn't deprived of sisterly love; he had never experienced it.

A bond between them started evolving when Mark moved to Washington, DC, where Mary Ellen now worked, to study architecture. The relationship was merely cordial until their father died. He was their genetic link, since they had different mothers. Their shared grief over the loss of their father helped them feel empathy for each other. They were, in fact, co-regulating, and filling in the emotional gaps that characterize privation. When she became seriously ill, he was by her side every day and nursed her until she passed away. Then, instead of experiencing privation, he experienced deprivation of sisterly love.

In short, privation doesn't have to be a permanent state. Our brains are plastic and emotional learning can occur throughout life. What we require to do that is the opportunity to create new experiences that regroove us, even erasing traumatic memories that have blocked us from healthy intimate relationships.

Therapists who have privated clients take a deliberate approach to creating new experiences to override the old ones. What Mark and Mary Ellen discovered over their years together is a form of the kind of therapeutic change an EFT clinician would deliberately orchestrate.

REACTION/CO-REGULATION

The attachment questionnaire suggests ways you might react in various circumstances depending on your attachment style. But human responses don't fit neatly into a causality model, that is, if *X* happens, then *Y* always occurs. Fortunately, human beings are not as simple and predictable as that. We don't necessarily respond to the same emotional stimulus from our partner exactly the same way every time. Reactions could be either amplified or mitigated depending on the extent to which one's partner either counters or supports co-regulation.

Co-regulation is a dynamic process between two beings that allows them to communicate and connect in ways that words alone do not express. It has both a physiological and a psychological component. We'll explore both here so that you see not only how it works, but also how to make it work in your relationship.

The Sympathetic Nervous System: Fight, Flight or Freeze

Susan was a fun-loving woman who wasn't annoyed by very much. She also had blind spots when it came to the little things in life, like not noticing that the pants she had on were covered with dog hair or that she had scratched her car with a grocery cart. Her first husband never seemed to notice—but then, he didn't notice much of anything she did and that was part of their problem. Susan next got involved with John, a man who paid a lot of attention to her. Early in their relationship, he made a point of admitting that he was fastidious about a lot of things, particularly since he was now a single dad to two school-age children. In that way, they were polar opposites: He cared about the details and he attended to them, whereas she didn't notice them. And that's one of the reasons why his kids adored her; she brought some flexibility to their daily lives.

About a year into their relationship—two months before they were scheduled to get married—she was chatting with a girlfriend as she pulled his new car into their garage. Without realizing it, she hit the garage door button twice, so it started to go up, and then it came crashing down on the hood of his Passat. John heard the crushing sound and rushed to the garage. She took one look at the disgust in his face and here's what happened:

- Her body went into overdrive, generating adrenaline—the stress hormone.
- Her body continued to ramp up, producing cortisol, a steroid hormone.
- Within milliseconds of these events, her sympathetic nervous system revved up. This is the part of the autonomic nervous system that rouses the body to action.
- Immediately on top of that, the adrenal gland that produced the stress hormone also produces DHEA (dehydroepiandrosterone), the most abundant steroid circulating in the body.

Susan was ready for fight or flight.

Commonly, people associate fight, flight, or freeze responses with a significant event such as being held up at gunpoint. But different people have
different thresholds for feeling fearful, as well as different reference points
regarding fear. Basically, from the momentous to the relatively insignificant,
anything that puts a person on "red alert" automatically activates the sympathetic nervous system so the body is ready for action. In our most crucial and
intense relationships—those we have with our partner, children, family members, and maybe even with very close friends—when our bond is attacked, we
react with flight, fight, or freeze.

Let's speculate that Susan's father had an explosive temper and she saw the
same look on John's face that her father had prior to an outburst. Even though
she has no direct reason to think that John might react violently, just seeing
that look would be enough to trigger a fear response. If John clenched his fist
or started storming toward the car, then that would signal an active threat. "A
dirty look," on the other hand, might be a cause of high anxiety, but certainly
not fear—right? Wrong. The sympathetic nervous system doesn't differentiate between what a person recognizes as the symbol of a threat—in this case,
a look of disgust—and a real, physical threat.

For Susan, the occurrence of the garage door smashing down on the car
gave her an instant, intense fear that she was in big trouble with John. She
had been careless beyond anything she'd done previously in their relationship. She could not predict his anger, and she was genuinely afraid of what
he might do. It was the *anticipation* of a threat that fueled the production of
those fight-or-flight hormones.

John saw the fear in her eyes and extreme tension in her body and knew
his initial response to the event was the cause. He took a deep breath, walked
to the driver's side of the car and asked, as calmly as he could, "Are you all
right, sweetheart?" She started to sob uncontrollably; he opened the door and
hugged her, triggering her parasympathetic nervous system.

The Parasympathetic Nervous System: Calm Down and Connect

What John did is something that Trevor guides people toward in EFT therapy
all the time: co-regulation. It is using a connection with another person to
reduce fear and arouse the parasympathetic nervous system, the other "half"
of the autonomic nervous system. In other words, just as automatically as
Susan got revved up, she was as automatically calmed down when she felt a
connection with John.

The parasympathetic nervous system allows a person to "rest and digest."
Blood pressure decreases, the pulse rate slows down, and normal bodily functions, such as digestion, can occur.

Even in the middle of an argument, if one member of a couple openly invites and gives a hug, it's possible to activate the parasympathetic nervous system and shift into a lower gear where conversation is possible.

We are chemistry. We are neurons. Sometimes, especially in an intimate relationship, we don't decide what's next; we feel what's next.

POINTS TO CONSIDER

Your family of origin informs your attachment style, and that attachment style is something you bring into your blending family. But neurological pathways aren't static. As your intimate, couple's relationship matures, you can regroove.

Also be aware that your children and stepchildren have already developed attachment styles. Be aware of them and sensitive to them, but also realize that these kids can regroove, too. Whether you are a biological parent or a stepparent, you will very likely be part of that evolution.

And remember: People can be taught to love.

NOTES

1. Vivien Prior and Danya Glaser, *Understanding Attachment and Attachment Disorders,* Jessica Kingsley Publishers, 2006.

2. Martha Stout, *The Sociopath Next Door,* Harmony, 2006, p. 6.

3. Paul A. Aiken, PhD, "Privation: Winnicott's Forgotten Concept: Application to Contemporary Psychoanalytic Treatment," August 2001, p. 2; http://www.academia.edu/5271034/Privation_Winnicotts_Forgotten_Concept_Application_to_Contemporary_Psychoanalytic_Treatment.

4. Paul A. Aiken, Unpublished essay, October 21, 2014.

Chapter 2

Understanding Parenting—and Stepparenting—Styles

Parents are always older, kinder, and wiser than their children.
Just get it right 30 percent of the time.
The role of a parent has a lot of power in it. Honor that reality, don't abuse it.

Trevor's top principles of parenting

There are two basic ways to consider how attachment styles relate to parenting styles. The first reflects what the parent is *actually* doing and the second, what the children *think* the parent or stepparent is doing.

Good news runs throughout this chapter. Much of it has to do with the efforts people of all attachment styles make to be good parents or stepparents; the efforts themselves can hold a lot of value even though the execution leaves something to be desired. This relates to Trevor's number two principle given above. Daniel Stern, who was a well-known psychiatrist specializing in infant development, talked about the "attunement" of a child's main caregiver and how it played a key role in developing a secure attachment style. By attunement, he meant the parent's or other caregiver's sensitivity to the verbal and non-verbal cues of a child, and the person's ability to put himself or herself into the mind of the child.[1] Some of Stern's work greatly upset some mothers (and fathers) who immediately wondered what they were doing wrong, not what they were doing right. Other therapists, such as Daniel Sonkin (*Learning to Live without Violence*), jumped into the discussion, bringing research that supports Trevor's "30 percent rule."

When a parent has good emotion regulation skills (sensitivity to his or her own emotions, and those of others) they are more likely to put those skills to use with their infant. This doesn't mean that secure parents are 100% attuned. Just the

17

opposite: The most secure parents are only about 30% attuned. However, they also know how to repair misattunements.[2]

Based on the results of the Chapter 1 questionnaire—and that's all it is, not an official test instrument—you have a sense of your adult attachment style as it pertains to your romantic life. This is a great foundation for you to understand yourself even though your attachment style as a parent may be somewhat different. In fact, one concept we explore later in the chapter is that parents and stepparents who may have insecure attachment styles with their partner can veer toward a more secure style with kids. Or vice versa.

PARENTING BEHAVIORS AND ATTACHMENT STYLES

In a highly competitive culture such as the one that exists in many parts of the United States, doting parents are common. We say "many parts" because there are still plenty of environments where kids are encouraged, but not pushed; hugged and applauded for achievements, but not given a trophy for just showing up.

Many parents and stepparents with loving intentions take their attentiveness to an extreme when it comes to "preparing" children to get into good schools so that they can "succeed" in life. They are sometimes neither preparing a child for the rigors of life, nor do they have a grasp of what success is outside of academic and materialistic measurements. They aren't necessarily bad parents, but they practice some bad parenting.

Dismissive parents—and studies have indicated this is more of a male tendency[3]—are focused on their own assault on the world of commerce, activism, or invention. They basically ignore their children at the same time they have high performance expectations for them. One might imagine someone highly competitive and financially successful like Donald Trump saying sincerely, "Just follow my lead!" and then going to the office to conquer the world. Someone like that might think that the greatest parenting is planting footsteps in the soil that the child can follow. We've seen this behavior with politicians, artists, and all kinds of driven individuals of both genders.

Dismissive parents, also known as avoidant parents, tend to have a military-style emphasis on following the rules. This style of parenting is not about a child's growth as much as it is about doing things right. Talking about emotions—simply asking, "How do you feel about this, Bobby?"—would be a foreign concept to them.

This is extremely dangerous for the child, and we might even call it a type of emotional abuse. If you have an avoidant attachment and parenting style, the trouble you have identifying your own emotions will likely translate into an inability to help your child identify his emotions. You would have a tendency to dismiss his experience with a get-on-with-it attitude. By doing that, you are robbing your child of the tools he needs to be resilient—to know what he's feeling, explain where it hurts and where he feels joyful, and be unafraid to express those things.

A dismissive parenting style is characterized by rigidity. A likely outcome is that the kid becomes rebellious, which is what can also happen with an anxious parenting style. When the child is old enough to feel either hemmed in by rules or smothered by a doting, worried parent, that child could explode emotionally and decide, "I've had enough!" Alternatively, some kids simply emulate their parents and they become just as rigid and avoidant or just as anxious and doting.

The "Donald Trump" type might be a loving and attentive husband, and the doting parent might be a joyful, adventuresome wife. That pattern of relating to a romantic partner may not be a predictor of parenting styles. Also, parenting styles aren't going to be consistent every moment of the week any more than a style of relating to a love partner. You have a dominant attachment style—and it's critical to know what it is—but you also need to realize that deviations from that style will occur. Sometimes we call that a "slip" and other times we call that a "breakthrough."

Any parent, for example, will be anxious (that is, "fearful" in some attachment theory nomenclature) at least part of the time, but that doesn't constitute a parenting style. An anxiously attached parent will hover; this describes the so-called helicopter parent, who tends to micromanage a child's life. Some of these parents who are overly involved in the child's life will do his homework because they are so anxious about the child making mistakes. This behavior comes out of a loving place, but it's misguided; it does not teach resiliency.

For her book, *Refeathering the Empty Nest*, psychotherapist Wendy Aronsson posed a couple of questions about doting parenting as part of an online survey. She asked: "How involved are you in your child's/stepchild's life?" and "How involved is your partner?" An overwhelming 97 percent of respondents indicated either a very high or relatively high level of involvement.[4] It's an important sign of the times, with it becoming increasingly more common for parents to insert themselves into a child's academic and social life. But just because it's common doesn't make it a good behavioral choice.

Trevor was getting her hair done one day when a woman in the chair next to hers told her stylist about a school project her son had done. "My son is in first grade, and we couldn't believe the assignment he got. It was a set of instructions that was pretty complicated."

She said he completed the work, left it on the dining room table, and then went to bed. The woman woke up in the middle of the night, worried about what her son had done. She looked it over and then redid it.

The boy took his mother's "superior" work to school the next day. Please note: Everything about what this mother did is wrong in this instance. We won't pull back from that condemnation of her parenting at that moment in time; in fact, she might also realize that what she did undermined her child's development. If so, she could fix her "misattunement."

In contrast, a secure mom would have asked what the project was about and invited her son to talk about it. She might ask, "How do you feel about what you've done?" and "Is there anything I can do to help?" A secure child would admit being satisfied with his work, or scared that it isn't quite up to par. He might say to his mom, "I don't really understand question five. Can you just help me with that one?"

Parents who make the child's experiences only about successes embed emotional deficits in the child's life. He has no chance to find out about being loved for himself instead of what he does. This kind of parenting also doesn't honor the natural progression involved in a child finding out who he is in relation to other people, and what he's capable of on his own.

In her practice, Trevor has seen the result of highly anxious parenting and it includes gravely negative outcomes like bulimic or anorexic children. They feel as though nothing they do is good enough and may give into destructive tendencies like not eating more than 1000 calories a day, because that gives them a sense of power over their own life. A mother of an anorexic teenager, as well as a preteen who also displayed traits of self-abuse, told Trevor, "I just can't handle this. When they were little, I could control everything they did. Now, I don't know what to do." Clearly, the mom's anxious attachment style led to her anxious parenting, making control of her children's behavior of greater importance than emotional connection with her kids.

Consider how easy it would be for a well-intentioned stepparent to move toward this kind of anxious parenting. Desperately wanting to "do it right" might drive an otherwise secure individual to step over the line and help too much, do too much, and stress out too much. This might be particularly pronounced with someone who has no biological children and who, therefore, hasn't gone through any of the early growth stages between infancy and preschool.

Blending also involves reacting to the partner's parenting style. If the biological dad makes it clear that it's vital that someone watch every second of his kids' soccer games and hover over their homework, then the stepmom might feel she has no choice if she wants to support his parenting, please him, and keep peace. Until she finds her footing in the household, she might exhibit features of anxious parenting, even though it's not consistent with what she thinks is best for the children.

Blending might also give rise to a type of chaotic parenting that is fraught with uncertainties, mixed messages, and inconsistent displays of affection. By its nature, blending is often characterized by some misunderstandings and mismatches that may not come into play in a biological family—or at least not as much. A kind of come-close-to-me, go-away-from-me parenting could be part of the daily confusion in some blending families.

Jane seemed comfortable raising her first two children. She and her husband Scott wanted, and planned for, just two children. Scott died in a head-on collision when the girls were three- and five-years-old. Within a year, she married one of Scott's closest friends, Todd. He wanted at least one biological child, so Jane reluctantly agreed to try to get pregnant. Even before their son Jamie was born, she referred to him as "the negotiated baby."

She had the normal feelings of protection and caring imbued by biology, and they were strengthened by an outpouring of affection from Jamie's half sisters and his father. Jane never completely adjusted, though, and her parenting was rather inconsistent. Sometimes, she seemed as loving and attentive as she had been with her girls; other times, it was almost as if he was a bother.

Years later, both of the grown-up girls went to other states for college and then settled into their own lives away from their parents' home. Jamie, who is now 22, has gone to four colleges and never got past his sophomore year. He moved back home and, even though he supposedly has a high IQ, does odd jobs and, for the most part, depends on his parents for financial support. It would be unfair to attribute all of Jamie's erratic behavior to Jane's chaotic parenting, but he certainly didn't benefit by not knowing where he stood with his mother on a day-to-day basis.

On a very sad note, Kitty Menendez, mother of Lyle and Eric, told her psychiatrist that she thought her sons were sociopathic before they murdered her and her husband, entertainment executive Jose Menendez, in 1989. Erik and Lyle were convicted in a high-profile trial that resulted in life imprisonment for both of them. Mental health professionals who have looked closely at the Menendez family history have concluded that a disorganized attachment style seemed to dominate interactions between Kitty and her sons: "In their case, it seems possible that the inconsistency and incoherence of Kitty and Jose's parenting styles may have been at fault for their son's aggressive tendencies."[5] Obviously, this is an extreme case, but every parent needs to sharpen his or her awareness of how profoundly parenting styles can affect a child's emotional development.

Parenting styles naturally change a bit as a child gets older. When your child is an infant, you are controlling every part of his life. It's not necessarily anxious parenting; it's the kind of attentive parenting that's required with a helpless baby. As the child gets older, there are minutes in the day when the child is in control; maybe it's a simple matter of choosing what toy to play with. As time goes on, the minutes turn to hours, and then days, and at some point you realized your "job" is done. You'll always be a parent, but you're done with parenting.

A toddler will take a few steps, stop, and then look over her shoulder to make sure her attachment figure is nearby. Then she'll run back. It doesn't take long for her to go a little further, and then even further. A securely attached child is able to explore and then come back. And when the child takes a few steps and falls, she'll look to mommy or daddy for a response. The parent with a secure style will provide comfort as well as confidence about taking a few more steps. "I'm here for you!" is followed by helping the child understand that sometimes we fall, so let's figure out how to stay upright the next time.

A secure parent will help the child name the experience she's having—both the event and the emotion associated with it. If you start when she's little, by the time she's a teenager her resiliency would have matured. She can tell you, "Mom, I didn't get invited to Taylor's party and I'm really hurt," instead of storming in the house, going to her room, shutting her door and never telling you why she's upset.

A toddler who is anxiously attached would cling to the attachment figure. When he takes a few steps away and falls, the anxiously attached parent would yelp, "Oh my God! Are you all right?!?" The clear message to the child is, "You should stay by my side and not try anything that might hurt you." It's the opposite of what needs to happen.

Trevor was at the shopping mall and little boy running with all his might took a splat on the floor. The mom had two other kids in tow at the time. She walked over to him and said calmly, "Oh my goodness, are you okay?" He looked up at her and seemed comforted right away. An anxious mother would have fussed and overreacted. An avoidant mother would have said, "C'mon. Get up." But this mom did a great job of helping her son put what happened into context. She acknowledged it was a big fall and helped him get up. Then they sat down on a bench, and looking at his little face, she asked him how he felt. He told her, basically admitting in his own words that he was embarrassed more than anything. "Do you want a hug?" she asked. And then, all was well. They hugged and moved on down the mall.

This confident progression toward getting greater distance from the main attachment figures is a vital part of growing up. It's part of the process of *separation-individuation*. Although the evolution begins as soon as control starts to slip away from you as a parent, it typically revs up in adolescence. "Separation" refers to the transition toward autonomy. A teen has to have the ability to start walking away from parents—literally and figuratively. "Individuation" is a term coined by renowned psychologist Carl Jung and he explained it this way:

> The concept of individuation plays a large role in our psychology. In general, it is the process by which individual beings are formed and differentiated; in

particular, it is the development of the psychological individual . . . as a being distinct from the general, collective psychology. Individuation, therefore, is a process of *differentiation* . . . having for its goal the development of the individual personality.[6]

It might be logical to conclude that separation and individuation might best be accomplished by one of the following:

a. Rebellion against an anxiously attached parent.
b. Avoidant parenting that puts the child at arm's length emotionally at an early age.
c. A sense of distance from the family unit that engenders connections by choice, not connections by birth or circumstance.

No. All wrong. A key study on attachment styles and parenting concluded:

Although the process of individuation during the transition into young adulthood is characterized by increasing autonomy, independence, and detachment from family members, our findings suggest that individuation is facilitated by attachment rather than detachment. Representations of parents as supportive and nurturing are related not to dependence but to the capacity for individuation.[7]

In other words, the kids who have had the benefit of secure parenting are actually more likely to leave their parents—in a normal, healthy way—than the kids who had parents who were anxious, dismissive, or chaotic.

PERCEPTIONS OF PARENTING AND ATTACHMENT STYLES

You are eight years old. Your biological mom and new stepdad are having a disagreement about a family matter and are getting a bit emotional. You are there in the room, listening, but they are carrying on as though you aren't there. You don't like that. Your brain yells, "Hey! Why are you ignoring me? You guys knew I was here when you got together! If this is so darned important, then it's my business, too!"

If one were to ask the eight-year-old in this imaginary situation what he thinks of his parents, he might burst out with negatives like, "They don't care about me!" He might also say, "My mom doesn't care about me as much since she married Joe." Unless this sort of thing happens a lot, though, the child will probably forget it. It was a deviation, not part of a pattern of dismissive-avoidant parenting!

From a very young child's perspective, *everything* you do somehow relates to him or her. You are a "good" parent or caregiver if, the whole time you're with the baby, you are watching, cuddling, feeding, changing diapers, teaching, clothing, and singing lullabies. From a somewhat older child's perspective, like the eight-year-old in the scenario, only *much* of what you do somehow relates to him or her. You're a "bad" parent for the ten minutes he wanted your attention and you weren't giving it to him. Other than that, you're fine. That is, unless your parenting is truly insecure and you are ignoring the child often, excessively rigid or punitive, or persisting with the pattern of his infancy—making *everything* about him.

From a teenager's or young adult's perspective, your parenting can now be discussed, judged, and criticized. Patterns have been established, at least with the biological parent or whoever has been the most consistent caregiver. Whether kids of this age challenge you openly (and you can expect that), or keep it to themselves, they are questioning your parenting. They may be thinking, "Are you doing a good job? Did you give me what I needed to be all I can be?"

Questions like those may not form precisely in their head, but they are probably there in some form. Even in a mutually secure relationship—or as the study referenced above suggests, maybe particularly in a secure relationship—it's normal that teens and young adults start evaluating their parents with some objectivity.

That study is called "Attachment Styles and Parental Representations" and it provides intriguing insights into how young adults characterize their parents' parenting styles. It is classic research conducted by a notable team composed of Kenneth N. Levy, Department of Psychology, Clinical Psychology Doctoral Program, City University of New York; Sidney J. Blatt, Departments of Psychiatry and Psychology, Yale University; and Phillip R. Shaver, Department of Psychology, University of California, Davis. Shaver's work in the area of attachment theory is particularly well known.

The team had to do more than simply ask a group of college students how they would describe the parenting they got in terms of attachment style. They first had to have a strong sense of the attachment styles of the college students; in other words, they had to know "where they were coming from."

The team chose 101 male and 88 female subjects to participate, with a median age of 19. They were put into three groups based on the three styles in an attachment measure developed by Shaver and his colleague, Cindy Hazan of Cornell University: secure, avoidant, and anxious/ambivalent. Not too long before the study began, Kim Bartholemew of Stanford had developed a four-category model of assessment that covers the four categories we've been discussing and described in Chapter 1—secure, dismissing (avoidant), preoccupied (chaotic), and fearful (anxious). That instrument was later integrated into the study as well.

Just to be clear on how Shaver and Hazan sorted things out—since this is the foundation for much of the study's conclusions—they defined the three categories as follows:

Secure—Describe their romantic relationships as friendly, trusting, and happy. They accept their partners regardless of faults. They tend to have long and fulfilling relationships.

Anxious/Ambivalent—View love in an obsessive way, with strong need for constant reciprocation and validation, along with emotional highs and lows, and feelings of jealousy and strong sexual attraction.

Avoidant—Characterized as being afraid of intimacy, experiencing emotional highs and lows during relationships, along with much jealousy.[8]

Wind Goodfriend, a psychologist who contributes to the Science of Relationships website, has made it easy for us to anchor the differences between the types by linking them to the three main characters in *Harry Potter*:

Hermione Granger is a perfect example of the "secure" attachment style. Born of parents who are supportive without being suffocating, secure people are confident, feel free to express their emotions, and are happy to trust others. . . . (She) projects this style onto her own teenage experiments in love. When Ron repeatedly shows that he's too much of a chicken to ask her out, she promptly moves on to someone else (Viktor Krum). She's jealous when Ron starts dating a fellow classmate (Lavender), but she waits patiently for him to realize that she's a better choice.

Her object of affection, Ron Weasley, is . . . "anxious/ambivalent." The hallmark of parents who produce anxious/ambivalent kids is inconsistency. The Weasleys certainly love their children, but they are either screaming at them (for example, through the use of "howlers") or simply distracted and thus, basically absent. This leads to children who are unsure of where they stand in relationships, always yearning for love, but never confident that they'll actually get it. . . . Ron's relationship personality becomes one of jealousy, clinginess, and, above all, insecurity.

Finally, Harry displays what can be argued as the least healthy attachment style: fearful (or sometimes called "avoidant"). Harry's birth parents were certainly loving, but he never really knew them. Instead, his adoptive parents were cruel, abusive, and clearly disgusted by him. This leads to Harry's fearful style, which is that he pushes everyone else away, never believing relationships will bring him any comfort. Harry prefers to do everything by himself, something he proves each and every time he has to face a challenge. In relationships, he avoids admitting that he likes anyone, and when he can no longer deny it, his response is to do nothing.[9]

So, with thanks to Dr. Goodfriend, we are simply going to refer to the three groups as the Hermione, Ron, and Harry groups.

Participants in the study began their involvement by going through an assessment to determine what their attachment style was like. They ranked responses on a scale from "strongly disagree" to "strongly agree" to statements such as "My romantic partner makes me doubt myself" and "I do not often worry about being abandoned."

Then they were asked to describe their parents in terms of attachment (and this could include adoptive parents and stepparents). As you may have already guessed, the young adults' attachment styles tended to suggest how they described their parents—but there were also some surprises that ran counter to the team's initial hypotheses. It's helpful to keep in mind that, while children tend to emulate their parents' attachments styles, very young children can also exhibit different attachment styles with different parents.[10] And as they get older, children can also rebel against their parents' style. In some cases, therefore, what the young adults indicated about themselves and what they said about their parents was a close match, and in others, that was not at all the case.

Before we take a look at the study results, here's a casual questionnaire. The following concepts were woven into the study involving the students. Take a look at them from two perspectives: (1) how you describe yourself in terms of your parenting style and (2) how you think your child(ren) and stepchild(ren) would describe your parenting style. There might be a difference between how you think a biological child and a stepchild would describe you—and that's perfectly normal.

Parenting Questionnaire

First, check off which words you would use to describe your parenting style. Try not to think of isolated incidents, but rather patterns of behavior. You might want to do this several times, with your biological child(ren) in mind one time, and your stepchild(ren) in mind another.

Next, check off which words you think your child(ren) and stepchild(ren) would use to describe your parenting style. Again, think in terms of patterns of behavior. Of course, the fact is, a child might give huge weight to being screamed at a few times and would label you "punitive" even though that's not the way you behave most of the time.

- Affectionate
- Ambitious
- Malevolent
- Benevolent
- Cold
- Warm

- Constructive involvement
- Intrusive
- Intellectual
- Judgmental
- Negative
- Positive
- Nurturing
- Punitive
- Successful
- Weak
- Strong

There is nothing about this little questionnaire that is scored or related to a definitive determination of your parenting style. These are simply words that might help you focus on how you might characterize your parenting style *versus* how a child may see your parenting style. These are words similar to those the students in the study were asked to use to represent their parents.

Another dimension of the parent-child relationship that the students were asked to evaluate was how ambivalent they felt about their parents. In psychology, the concept of ambivalence is often described as an approach-avoidance relationship with someone or something. In this context, we might think of it as being drawn toward a parent sometimes and repelled by that parent at other times. The study participants used a 1-to-5 ranking to describe how ambivalent they felt.

Starting with a primary focus on the ambivalence assessment, here is a summary of how the different groups characterized the parenting styles of their mothers and fathers:

- Those in the Hermione group represented their mothers as significantly more benevolent and less punitive than did the students in the Ron or Harry groups.
- People in the Hermione group portrayed their mothers with less ambivalence.
- They also represented their fathers pretty similarly to their mothers.
- Ron group males expressed a lot of ambivalence in representing their mothers—much more than the other two groups. Note that this was distinctly associated with the men in that group; the women in the Ron group didn't nearly have the same level of approach-avoidance feelings as the men did.
- In contrast, it was the Harry group women who had the most ambivalence about their mothers.[11]

Let's break away from the summary to look at the meaning of the results so far. The study team fully expected what they got from the Hermione group:

positive representations of their parents and a relatively mature description of them and the relationship they have with them. In other words, they didn't feel ambivalence about the way they related to their parents; they felt consistency.

But the ambivalence ratings of the Ron group were surprises to them. Their hypothesis going into the study was that they would feel a lot more ambivalence about their parents than the Harry group, regardless of gender. They didn't expect to see gender differences, nor did they expect to see avoidant females having even more ambivalence than their anxious counterparts.

So are your boy children and your girl children experiencing your parenting styles in different ways? We wouldn't draw broad conclusions based on a single study, or multiple studies of small groups like this, but it is something for you as a parent to consider. What has your parenting experience suggested to you? Are the boys and girls in your household responding different to your discipline, affection, guidance, and encouragement?

People in the Ron group "view love in an obsessive way, with strong need for constant reciprocation and validation," according to the Shaver-Hazan description. It's easy to see, therefore, why the researchers would suspect that anyone in this group would express a lot of ambivalence about their parents: There was probably a pattern of giving and withdrawing affecting the parenting; the kids didn't know where they stood all the time.

But it's the females in the Harry group—"afraid of intimacy, experiencing emotional highs and lows during relationships"—that had the strongest approach-avoidance feelings about their parents. It's important to note that the Shaver-Hazan definition of avoidant is colored by fear, so we might actually have to relabel this group "fearful avoidant," whereas the attachment style we often associate with the avoidance might be called "dismissing avoidant." This would be the difference between someone who turns her back on intimacy because of fear of rejection and someone who turns her back on intimacy because her career is peaking.

The distinction is important in understanding how these two groups of women saw their parents. In many ways, women are socialized toward being anxious-ambivalent. We wouldn't say this about *all* women, because different races, cultures, and communities are not all going to have their girls' aspirations and personalities shaped by Disney princesses. However, the females in the study, recruited from the State University of New York at Buffalo, are representative of a mostly white, middle-class, or upper-middle-class group. With that in mind, we'd agree with the study team that society instills a sense of tentativeness about romantic relationships and how they need to be earned through certain behaviors. So whereas we might say that males in the Ron group were moved in that direction by a particular kind of parenting, it might not be as true for females of a similar background. Girls can get it from each other, from television, and from awful young-adult novels.

You might see a female child of yours change in the way she relates to you, as external influences in her life become more dominant. Your parenting may not have changed, but she seems different. The effects of socialization and the popular views of femininity in your community are having an impact. For example, Maryann interviewed a number of preteens and teenage girls about their involvement in extreme sports. In one session, she asked them why they left the skate park after the boys got there. After an embarrassing silence, one of the girls admitted that the boys made fun of them when they fell during a run. They wanted these boys to like them so they didn't want them making fun of them. Even with secure parenting, girls who are profoundly affected by the judgment of their peers may, for a while at least, give in to this Ron Weasley attachment style. Parents may see this as a silly phase they're going through, but it's real and it may be a "silly phase" that lasts for decades. The study team even went so far as to say that "there are similarities between traditional femininity and the anxious-ambivalent style."[12]

Here's the difference for the girl who develops a genuine fear of intimacy: It probably happened over time and was engendered by a persistent parenting style. That girl's expression of great ambivalence about her parents, or at least one of them, would seem to be a natural outcome.

For parents and stepparents in a blending family, the expressions of understanding on the part of the Ron group might be a particularly relevant result. You try to be consistent in your parenting and aim for a secure parenting style, but much of your home life is in a state of flux. You have anxiety, maybe on a daily basis, and it affects your parenting. Despite the upheavals and inconsistencies, the kids know you are there for them. They may be mad at you more than half the time—you're "malevolent and punitive" to use the study terms—but the bottom line is that they know you have their back.

To put it back in the Hogwarts context, even though Ron got a howler from his parents, if you'd asked him if they loved him, he would have said, "Of course." Even after getting screamed at, he didn't think they were horrible parents. (For those unfamiliar with *Harry Potter*, a howler is a magical letter that arrives in a red envelope. You have to open it or it will explode. When you open it, you get yelled at in the voice of the person who wrote the letter. After that, the howler bursts into flames.)

There is one more result that might be particularly useful in the context of a blending family. The study team differentiated between "continuously secure" and "earned secure." Continuously secure individuals have a narrative that describes benevolent and nurturing relationships from an early age. In contrast, the "earned secure" individuals have a narrative portraying difficult early relationships that they came to understand and/or explain. They essentially went from insecure to secure in terms of attachment style.

Let's speculate that the "difficult early relationships" encompass a parents' divorce, the remarriage of a biological parent, and having to adjust to a household with stepsiblings—but that's followed by a happy outcome of blending. Researchers have found that the earned secure individual were similar to insecure individuals in some respects, but were similar to continuous secure individuals with regard to good parenting behavior.[13]

Putting all clinical jargon aside, this featured study by Levy, Glatt, and Shaver is one of many that indicate that your sincere attempts to nurture a child are associated with that child's sense of autonomy, self-esteem, and perceived competence.

Try to get a handle on your own attachment style and then, as a parent/stepparent, just do your best to move toward a more secure style of both romantic and parental attachment.

POINTS TO CONSIDER

In many blended families, the transition from one household to another is hard for the kids because they encounter different styles of parenting. The demands they can feel on them might be extremely different in each setting. One family might be more anxious about things like homework and rules, whereas the other one might be very relaxed. A complicating factor could be like the one that Trevor faces: Her stepdaughter Eva spends weekdays with her and her biological father, but has most weekends with her biological mother. She goes from a school-oriented week where she shares the spotlight with two stepsiblings, to the relatively no-pressure weekend of being the sole beneficiary of mom's attention. All parents and stepparents involved in a scenario like this need to remember what the picture looks like from the child's point of view.

As a team, you and your partner might smooth out some of the bumps in the blending process if you have a sense of everyone's attachment style. We interviewed one family in which the stepmother had a secure attachment style and could accurately describe the attachment styles of everyone in her household because she is an EFT therapist. Her husband was avoidant and dismissive. One of her stepchildren was avoidant and fearful, and her stepdaughter was, as she says, "a full on pursuer/drama queen." You don't have to be a therapist to have, and act on, this basic understanding of how children tend to connect or disconnect from the people around them. It will help you move the entire family toward connection.

NOTES

1. Daniel Stern, *The Interpersonal World of the Infant,* Basic Books, 2000.

2. Daniel Sonkin interviewed by David DiSalvo for "Attachment Theory and the Brain: An Interview with Dr. Daniel Sonkin," *Neuronarrative*, January 12, 2009; https://neuronarrative.wordpress.com/2009/01/12/attachment-theory-and-the-brain-an-interview-with-dr-daniel-sonkin/

3. Kenneth Levy, Sidney J. Glatt, Phillip R. Shaver, "Attachment Styles and Parental Representations," *Journal of Personality and Social Psychology* 74 *(*1998): 407–419.

4. Wendy Aronsson, *Refeathering the Empty Nest*, Rowman & Littlefield, 2014, pp. 43–44.

5. http://www.psychwiki.com/wiki/PSY307-Attachment_Theory

6. Carl G. Jung, *Psychological Types (The Collected Works of C. G. Jung, Vol. 6) (Bollingen Series XX)*, Princeton University Press, 1976.

7. Ibid., Levy.

8. Fetzer Institute, "Original Attachment Three-Category Measure"; http://fetzer.org/sites/default/files/images/stories/pdf/selfmeasures/Attachment-OriginalAttachmentThreeCategoryMeasure.pdf.

9. Wind Goodfriend, "Attachment Styles at Hogwarts: Love in Harry Potter's World," Science of Relationships; http://www.scienceofrelationships.com/home/2011/7/8/attachment-styles-at-hogwarts-love-in-harry-potters-world.html.

10. Ibid.

11. Ibid.

12. Ibid.

13. J. Pearson, D.A. Cohn., P.A. and C.P. Cowen "Earned and continuous-security in adult attachment: Relation to depressive symptomatology and parenting style," *Development and Psychopathology* 6 (1994): 359–373.

Chapter 3

Key Challenges to the Blending Process

Judith chose a royal blue dress for her father's wedding. Lace lined with satin—she felt like a princess. "But this isn't about me," she thought. "It's about Dad and Dee."

Harry and Dee had first thought about getting married two years before, but figured that might be too much for their families; they'd wait until the time was right and everyone got to know one another. The wait made it hard on them, though. Dee was a devout Roman Catholic so they couldn't just "live in sin" and she didn't even feel comfortable taking trips alone with Harry.

The families would have to understand, they concluded. They wanted to marry; they needed to marry.

As Judith entered St. Joseph's Church on the day of the wedding, she looked around at the now-familiar faces of her step-relatives. For the past couple of years, they'd all made an effort to spend holidays as a family, and about half of them even spent a week vacationing together at Dee's time-share on the Florida coast. Now they were all together—for good. Judith walked into the middle of her new, expanded family: Her biological sister with her two children and husband, and Dee's six children, their spouses, thirteen grandchildren, and four great-grandchildren. Harry and Dee had both just turned 85.

As we found out from our interviews, surveys, and other research, blended families come in all shapes, sizes, and ages. The happy situation of Harry and Dee serves as a modern-day example of how commonplace mergers of all kinds of households are today and how blending often involves the needs, priorities, and sensibilities of multiple generations.

An important lesson out of the Harry and Dee story relates to the first point we make in this chapter about challenges to the blending process: While respecting the families they both already have, the couple has to put each other first. Even at the age of 85, Harry and Dee still had some emotional hurdles to get over in order to make it up the center aisle of St. Joseph's Church. Instead of making their relationship have a secondary role to parenting, though, it was taking a secondary role to grand-parenting and great-great-parenting!

The biggest challenge to the blending process is a marriage or partnership that allows the personal relationship of the couple to take a back seat to parenting. It's vital to keep the marriage in the front seat and keep the kids in the back. That doesn't mean ignoring a child's broken arm and taking off for a dinner date with the spouse, but it does mean a couple consistently seeing their relationship as a priority.

With that in mind, here are what we consider the top five challenges in the blending process:

- Putting the couple first
- Resolving parenting differences
- Communicating stability to the children
- Setting the boundaries of stepparenting
- Establishing equality where there is inequality

PUTTING THE COUPLE FIRST

In the movie *Blended*, Lauren and Jim, portrayed by Drew Barrymore and Adam Sandler, come to realize they like each other primarily because of how they interact with each other's children. Despite being repelled by each other on a blind date, they are later thrown together on an African vacation where they get to exhibit some lovely parenting skills. It's a typical Hollywood, upside down setup in which the willing suspension of disbelief gets us from an improbable premise to a believable, happy ending.

Probably the biggest stretch of imagination in this story is that Lauren and Jim don't like each other until they see each other as good parents. In reality, it's far more likely that a blended family begins with a romantic and/or sexual interest between two adults. The kids get worked into the couple's scenario rather than the couple getting worked into the kids' scenario.

But even if the beginnings of your blend were like that of Lauren and Jim, your intimate relationships with your partner must come first. The two of you are the core unit in this evolving family. Your choice to team up laid the emotional foundation for the merger of two households.

There are countless ways that couples may submerge the importance of their relationship in a blended household. And don't be fooled by the apparent simplicity of the concept: There are plenty of subtle and insidious ways that couples do this, remaining unaware of what they're doing or the impact it has on their union—and ultimately on their children and stepchildren as well.

Here's an example: Holly and Nate met at the local farmer's market one Saturday morning in June. When they began dating, they made a habit of meeting at the farmer's market whenever they were both in town; they joked about it being their favorite summertime date. After they got married, they continued their "date morning" until Holly's nine-year-old daughter asked if she could go along. They brought her along a couple of times and she kept asking to come back. She loved sampling the freshly baked cookies, organic peaches, and other treats. After four trips in which Holly's daughter came along, Nate started to find other things to do on Saturday morning. Going to the farmer's market wasn't a date anymore.

Holly and Nate had an easily fixable problem once they recognized it: Drop off Holly's daughter and her best friend at one end of the market, while Holly and Nate start at the other end and enjoy their time together. They would just meet up an hour later with the kids.

Gabby and Mark had a more serious issue, in part because Gabby had no experience of parenting and Mark really wanted to be done with it. When Gabby and Mark married, she brought no children to the relationship and he brought five, between ages 6 and 17. Mark's divorce had been acrimonious, largely because he connected with Gabby in the early days of the separation. Mark agreed that the three youngest children, a six-year-old boy and twin ten-year-old girls, would not spend time with him and Gabby at their home until they were older (a situation Trevor disagrees with. All kids need to bond, spending time with the biological and the stepparent at their home no matter what the age of the children is). The two teenagers did come for visits, however, because they wanted to—in part to get away from their mother's bitterness over the divorce. Knowing that the teens were coming to visit to get some peace and some dad time, Gabby went to great lengths to make sure the refrigerator was stocked with their favorite foods, the latest video games were loaded on the system, and that Mark had as few distractions as possible so he could focus on them during the visit. That arrangement worked fine as long as the visits were a few days here and there. Then, a little more than a year after their marriage, the younger teen asked if he could spend the summer with his dad and Gabby. It was an experience that nearly tore them apart. Having a child in the house every day meant that the privacy and spontaneity they had enjoyed was gone. They didn't realize it at first, but their relationship was emotionally starving.

After two months of having his son around daily, the friction was awful. Mark blew up at Gabby and said, "This marriage is starting to feel just like that last one!" Mark's son sensed the tension and felt like an intruder. He packed his bags and went back to his mother's house. Mark and Gabby went to a counselor and, fortunately, rediscovered their connection. But as of now, the fear persists: What will happen next time one or two of the kids come to stay? Will they ever be able to blend?

One exercise that an EFT therapist would use with a couple like Gabby and Mark involves focus on a "felt sense." Felt sense is the experience of your partner's feelings. This is the key to healing past hurts and to long-lasting connection. One partner has confidence that other feels her pain and joy. Using the concept of felt sense enables a couple to co-regulate—to soothe each other by engaging the parasympathetic nervous system, as we described in Chapter 1—because both understand the nature of the emotional support that the other needs.

A practical and beautiful dimension of the interaction is a somatic experience, which involves making a connection between your emotions and your body. It is the ability to identify exactly what you are feeling as well as where.

If you go to your doctor with a complaint about a pain, the doctor will ask you exactly where the pain is. You may point at a spot or describe a location inside your body. The question makes sense to you and giving the doctor an answer is a relatively straightforward exercise. Describing where you feel an emotion is not radically different from that, yet it's a foreign concept to most people.

For example, let's say Gabby has a tendency to hold tension in her shoulders and this was something that surfaced during one of their sessions with the therapist. A week later, Mark noticed that her shoulders were slightly elevated while she was asking about a holiday visit from Mark's two teenagers. Without even saying anything, he hugged her and the tension eased out of her shoulders. On a deep level, she felt understood and comforted.

This is a simple experience of co-regulation. These two people don't just feel love *for* each other; they feel love *in* each other. Many couples discover this on their own and don't have a name for it. They simply enjoy it year after year. EFT therapists like Trevor spark the awareness of felt sense in a couple and then help them use it to "re-couple."

In a blended household, with its unique stresses and, perhaps, many unexpressed expectations, the use of felt sense to bring a couple to a connected state is invaluable! Here is guidance on how to cultivate an awareness of the link between emotion and body:

1. Imagine a joyous moment you've shared with your partner. Maybe it was your wedding. Maybe it was a great laugh you had during a vacation together. Where do you feel the emotion of that moment in your body? How does a vivid recall of that moment affect your:
   a. Breathing

   b. Facial muscles
   c. Posture
   d. Tension level
2. Imagine a moment in direct contrast to that—a time when you felt under attack. You and your partner were in conflict and you wondered if the relationship would make it. Where do you feel the emotions of that moment in your body? How does a vivid recall of it affect your:
   a. Breathing
   b. Facial muscles
   c. Posture
   d. Tension level
3. Imagine a moment when you and your partner disagreed about something, but you worked it out. It might have been something tough, like figuring out how you would manage visitation rights and finances with the biological parent of a child in your home. What happened between the two of you to defuse the tension? What did you say and do with each other that brought you together in your thoughts as well as your feelings?
   a. Did you touch?
   b. Did you feel empathy for the other person?
   c. How did you show you were trustworthy?
   d. Did you feel as though you were in this together and had each other's back?

"Putting each other first" necessarily involves using the concept of felt sense to help with your co-regulation as a couple. You may be doing that now and calling it something like "an us moment" or "hug time." It doesn't matter what you call it as long as you integrate it into your lives.

With felt sense as the foundation of putting each other first, you can deal much more effectively with the day-to-day challenges of blending.

A practical, even mundane, way of putting each other first also relates to routine communication. With all of the mobile tools we have at hand to get time-sensitive messages across, it's easy to slip into an attitude of efficiency with a partner. You might text: "Stuck in mtg. Pls pick up Josh at 3." You could end it with eight more letters and a punctuation mark: "Thx!Love".

Sometimes the "Thx" is the most important part of that message. One of the stepmothers we interviewed had had a particularly rough time with her stepdaughter when she was 14. The young teen had been living with them full-time for a year at that point and she often showed how unaccustomed she was to discipline. The stepmom navigated the challenges beautifully and showed her stepdaughter she was there for her. We asked her if that brought her closer to her husband, the girl's biological father. "Not really. It didn't separate us, but it didn't bring us any closer."

"Did he ever thank you?" we asked.

"For what?" she asked.

"For stepping up to a pretty big challenge and doing a great job of parenting his child."

She went silent. Finally, she said, "No, he thought it was my duty. But if he had said 'thank you' occasionally, I think that would have brought us closer together."

Part of putting each other first is paying attention to ways that your partner goes well beyond "duty," out of love and respect for you. Expressing appreciation is a vital element of a healthy intimate connection.

RESOLVING PARENTING DIFFERENCES

A big challenge also comes out of the parents/stepparents not backing each other up in parenting matters. Each household has different rules, with some having almost no rules when it comes to homework, computer use, staying up late, and so on. And going back to attachment/parenting styles, different parents naturally have different approaches to household rules as well as ways of responding to rule-breaking. In one situation we heard about, the biological mom yelled when her daughters disobeyed, but took zero punitive action. In contrast, when her children visited their biological dad and stepmom, there was structure and discipline, but no yelling. Key challenges to the blending process center on those kinds of differences and how the two people who merged the households handle them. The bottom-line question is: Do they handle them as a team, or not?

Jan and Pete had four children, ages 7 through 10, when they merged their households. There was a good deal of interaction between the ex-spouses and Jan and Pete since all four adults were actively involved in co-parenting. And then along came a fifth influence as well: Pete's former wife's new boyfriend, who didn't seem to understand that he should back off from trying to parent Pete's son.

Even while she and Pete were managing a household where there were four children 50 percent of the time, Jan worked full-time as a consultant with a specialty in strategic planning. It served her and the family well. She took the long view: She could see she and Pete should lay out some ground rules for themselves as otherwise the differences in parenting styles could be a source of massive confusion for the kids. Whenever they did not agree on a way to handle something, they went "offline" with the kids, rather than try to give a quick answer. They gave themselves a moment to address two questions: "What will the children lose from making this decision?" and "What will the children gain from making this decision?"

They found their decisions becoming more focused on the big picture—the emotional health of all the children—and not the little stuff, like how many minutes of computer use were okay for a ten-year-old. Those little things seemed to have more of a context just by asking those two questions.

Jan and Pete also made conscious choices about certain rules and practices in light of their two big questions. They made a list of the rules that would be the same for all kids, regardless of their ages, as well as the things that had to do with age-appropriate behavior and choices. They had to revisit the items on the list, of course, as time moved on and technology got more complicated with, for example, new forms of social media.

COMMUNICATING STABILITY TO THE CHILDREN

Secure parents help their children organize their thoughts about events and emotions. In a general sense, they communicate stability by letting them know they are heard, helping them express ideas and emotions that are difficult to express, and letting them know they are there for them even in tough times. Even moms and dads with children in a refugee camp can communicate stability to their children.

Here's the principle in action in an ordinary way. Maryann saw a tourist family in the local grocery store. (If you've ever lived in a "destination location," you know how easy it is to spot a tourist family.) The children were probably 1, 4, and 6 and they were obviously excited to be on vacation; it may have been their first day in the Rocky Mountains. The little boy of about 4 was looking at his mom and moving his arms all around him. Small trowels, claws, and other gardening implements suddenly flew off of a wire spinner rack as the child connected with it. The noise alone must have frightened him and he plopped himself down on the floor and seemed to experience a mixed-up sense of guilt, anger, fear, and embarrassment.

His mother got down on her knees to his level, looked him straight in the eyes, and said, "I know it was an accident. Are you okay?" He nodded. Her tone of voice was calm and completely devoid of judgment: "Let's just pick these things up and hang them up again, okay?" He took her hand and got up. With a lot of enthusiasm, he had his new project: hanging implements that had fallen on to the lowest branches of the display rack. Neither mom nor dad acted as though the process had to be rushed, and the older sister didn't hesitate to help.

By the time you meet your stepchildren, they have probably gone through something like this and, depending on the parenting style of the biological parent who was there at the time, the child either got a secure message—like this one—or an insecure message. The secure message conveys a sense to the child that the connection with that parent is stable. An insecure message could have been a punitive response: "What the hell have you done!?! Pick up everything right now!" Or, it might have been an anxious response: "My poor baby! Did any of those things hurt you?" Or, it might have been the kind of avoidant response that teaches kids how to get away with things: "Let's go, Chad! Someone else will take care of this." With an insecure communication, the child is likely left feeling unsteady, perhaps full of fear or anger, or maybe just a sense that it doesn't matter how careless or irresponsible he is.

Communicating stability to children begins with honest communication between the couple. They have to set an example of openness, consistent respect for truth-telling, and a practice of active listening.

Active listening is a full-bodied, mindful way of demonstrating to someone that you care about what that person is saying. It's an essential skill for a couple and an essential skill of parenting. It makes a person of any age feel respected—and there is a tremendous sense of comfort and connection in that. Let's first look at the mechanics of active listening and then the practice of it.

Active listening has physical, intellectual, and emotional components.

Intellectual: You listen for keywords, which might be indicated by emphasis or how frequently they are used. For example, if your teenager talks about Spanish class a lot, but doesn't seem to be getting any better speaking Spanish, maybe he's trying to share with you that there's someone in Spanish class who's particularly interesting to him.

You also want to listen for words that aren't there, but you would expect them to be there. For example, you ask that same teen how soccer practice went and he talks about the new jerseys and the team schedule for the season. What you "hear" from that is the omission of anything about practice. Maybe it was awful for some reason, perhaps because he did something really embarrassing and doesn't want it to come up in conversation. It could be the very thing he should be talking about, though, so he can get over it. It doesn't mean you should prod when you detect a possible omission, but your attentiveness might trigger a desire for him to tell you more.

Physical: What you do and what you don't do with your body, including your voice, can signal the other person that you are listening carefully. Your posture, gestures, focus, energy, tone of voice, pace of speech, and word choices can either reassure someone that you're listening and not judging, or they can shut the other person down.

To start, invitational body language involves looking at the person you're talking with. If you ask your child a question and then put your focus on your cell phone, that's not the body language of active listening. In fact, you shouldn't even be holding a cell phone if you want to show your child that you're really listening. You also want to remove or minimize barriers between you. If you're both sitting at a table, lean into it so the table seems more like shared real estate than an object that's separating you.

Your vocal patterns should be whatever is normal for you when you're not under stress. In other words, if your child is telling you something that is emotionally charged, if you want to use active listening encourage her to tell you the whole story, then try to keep tone of voice and pace of speech as even as possible. It's in these tough conversational moments that active listening is an invaluable tool to communicate stability and engender trust.

Babies are sensitive to physical appearance and presentation, too, and will communicate more when they see and hear particular signals. Infants start to identify voices and faces very early on—just a few hours after they are born—and they respond well to "infant-directed speech." Studies have shown that babies prefer communication that involves the kind of slow, melodic speech that characterizes so-called baby talk; it helps them understand the caregiver's emotional intentions, as well as to learn language.[1] They will also stay tuned into the person longer if she has a happy look on her face rather than a fearful or neutral one.[2]

Emotional: Listening to your child or stepchild share events and feelings with you is bound to arouse some kind of emotional response. It could just be simple pride in knowing that you and she connect well enough to have a conversation. Even though you want your tone and pace to be normal while you're listening, at some point, it's great to show how you feel. Your child will have some assurance that you really were listening and that you care about what she told you.

Ann's stepdaughter, Sammie, came back home a few hours before her scheduled weekend with her mother was supposed to end. They'd had a fight about where she hoped to go to college after she finished high school the following year. She stormed up the stairs and closed her bedroom door. Ann called up the stairs: "Sammie, can I get you anything?" Silence.

After resuming her work on a legal brief she was preparing, Ann realized that Sammie was standing in the doorway. She wasn't crying, but it looked as though she had been. Ann said, "I need a break from this. Want to join me in the kitchen for a brownie?"

Over brownies, Sammie began by complaining bitterly about her biological mother trying to tether her. She had told her daughter she would fight with everything possible to keep her in the United States for college—actually the East Coast of the United States—even though Sammie had her eyes on the University of Sussex.

Ann asked her to start at the beginning, since they'd never talked much about Sammie's college aspirations: "Tell me what got you interested in

Sussex." Sammie went on for twenty minutes, with Ann occasionally making a remark like "I didn't know that" or "How interesting!" as she learned about why Sammie thought it would be a great place to study chemistry. The conversation became far more about what Sammie wanted to do "when she grew up" than about her mother's lack of support and understanding. Eventually, Sammie blurted out that she realized her mom was just scared of losing her. Ann smiled and complimented her stepdaughter on being so insightful. She said, "I'd miss my daughters, too, if they moved to another country."

What Sammie got out of Ann's active listening was a sense of an adult, mother-figure respecting her thoughts and her dreams. And she did it without any implication of criticism of her biological mother. In fact, she allowed a little empathy to flow out by admitting that she would have a hard time if her daughters made the same choice.

Sammie's "Thanks for the brownie" was really a much more encompassing expression of gratitude and Ann knew that. The future chemist went upstairs and promptly called her mom to reconnect in a positive way.

Another way to communicate stability is through family practices. Jan and Pete, mentioned above, offered some excellent advice for blended families (it's something that has served them well): As early in the blending process as you can, establish your own rock-solid traditions as a family. They warned that it can be complicated, particularly if you center it on an occasion like Thanksgiving or a birthday, but it doesn't have to be.

The first thing they did as a new family was just meant to be a short vacation. It was a weeklong road trip, but everyone enjoyed it so much that it became a tradition for the next eight years. That first year, they rented a minivan and drove down the Pacific coast from Oregon to Southern California. They stayed in inexpensive motels and ate at diners. Another year, another road trip with more cheap hotels and diners. The entire family had fun figuring out where the next one would be.

Communicating stability is about giving children a sense of safe haven—for their thoughts, emotions, and general well-being. Simple tools like active listening and blended family traditions can go a long way toward sustaining that.

SETTING THE BOUNDARIES OF STEPPARENTING

Cara got along well with her young stepdaughters, ages 2, 5, and 6 when she met them. In fact, they started teasing her that they wanted to call her "mom" or some variation of it. She said, "You already have a mom. My name is Cara." This is something that Trevor feels is very important in the blending process: One of the boundaries is making it clear that the child has biological parents and the step is not a substitute for the biological parent; that includes, in most cases, ensuring that the child names one mother and one father.

Cara's popularity with the children prompted them to do something very creative in naming her. Their father was "daddy." Their mother was "mommy." So, they thought it was only fitting that their nice stepmom have a name that "rhymed." They have called her "Carrie" ever since.

When Demi Moore married Ashton Kutcher, who apparently still has a good relationship with Moore's three daughters, they reportedly called him MOD—"my other dad." Another approach some families have taken is to combine the stepparent's first name with "dad" or "mom," as in "Jimdad." In some cases, it wouldn't exactly roll of the tongue, but in others, it might work just fine. The nicknames are a clear illustration of the boundary between the role of the biological parent and that of the stepparent.

Boundaries start with the stepparent's realization that when you are co-parenting stepchildren, you may love them, but you may not love them the same way you love your own biological children. There is a need to try to achieve equity and fairness within the blend, of course, but there is probably a difference in the way you feel toward your biological children and your stepchildren. That's normal. Setting boundaries supports your efforts to create a blended household where everyone feels as though home is a safe haven despite the differences in family of origin.

In addition to the caution against allowing a stepchild to call you mom or dad, we recommend some boundaries, which can be categorized into information, discipline, financial, and behavioral boundaries.

Information boundaries

These are various lines that should not be crossed when children move back and forth from one parent's household to another's.

- Never use your children as conduits of information between you and an ex.
  You don't want to send your child out the door to spend a weekend with dad and say, "Tell him we have a conference with your math teacher on Wednesday afternoon." It's your responsibility to work out a system of communication with the other biological parent of your child. Fortunately, mobile devices make it easy to send an email or text, so there is no need to put the child in the middle of the information exchange.
- Do not pump your kids for information about an ex.
  Sometimes kids will volunteer information, which is essentially tattling. When they blurt out a juicy fact, shut it down with something like "I know your mom is dating Jim and that's nice. But that's her business. Let's talk about something else." The exception to this is if the child feels unsafe

at the other house for some reason and expresses that to you. Examples might be a pattern of alcohol or drug use that seriously impairs the parent or someone else in the household. There is a flip side to this: As part of a power play, some kids will try to suggest a parent was mean or abusive to play one parent against another. You need to listen and try to evaluate objectively whether the child has a legitimate concern.

- Do not speak ill about an ex in front of that person's child.

Maryann once heard a mother say to her young adult daughter, a friend of Maryann's: "I was pregnant with you when your father started running around with that bimbo he married." The kids are half of each biological parent, so by slamming an ex, the child feels slammed as well. The daughter snapped back: "Well dad invited me to live with him in Hawaii and I've decided I'm going."

No child, not even one that's nearly adult, should have to hear vitriolic remarks about a parent from the other parent—or from a stepparent. Some kids have an amazing capacity to shut out what they don't want to hear. Others plunge into depression; when people they love don't get along, they are deeply upset. Still others get angry. In some cases, it's anger aimed specifically at one or both parents and in other cases, the child becomes angry at the world.

- Maintain an information boundary between the ex and your blended family.

One family that had just begun blending sought counseling from Trevor. The biological father had made the mistake of telling what he thought was a funny story to his ex about a misguided attempt his fiancée had made to bond with the eight-year-old daughter. The fiancée was trying very hard to develop a relationship with the little girl and did something silly. By sharing the story with the ex-wife, he essentially threw his bride-to-be under the bus and put his relationship with her in jeopardy.

The ex also has no business calling the stepparent on the basis of it being in the child's best interest. It's an intrusion on the blended home. The biological parent needs to tell the ex that conversations can happen between the two of them, but that no one should call the stepparent with advice or complaints. The stepparent needs to feel backed up, appreciated, and protected. One of the stepmoms we interviewed said her husband's ex called after every visit the kids made and yelled at her. The stepmom did not let it bother her because she felt her marriage was on solid ground and the ex yelling periodically was simply a desperate gesture to try to make her miserable.

- Do not expose the kids to conversations about finances and other private matters pertaining strictly to your household.

Adult conversations and events that happen in your house need to stay in your house between the two of you. If a parent does not pay child support, for example, that is not the child's problem nor is it the child's responsibility to fix it. Restricting visitation rights over support payments is a way of having an adult concern leak out of the house even if you don't explicitly tell the child what's going on. He will either be told by the other parent or figure it out that "no money" means "no relationship." That is completely unfair and turns the child into a pawn.

Nonpayment of support or agreed-upon tuition payments can cause high emotions and stress for the blended family. When kids are in their late teens and their biological parent is not paying child support or tuition, you may communicate what is going on in a nonemotional way. Older kids are able to take in the truth. Try not to blame and criticize your ex-spouse in the process. Simply be clear. Seek professional help if this becomes a disruptive issue in your family.

Discipline boundaries

The first piece of guidance is to check with the biological parent before disciplining stepchildren. The second is to have clear rules on what constitutes good and bad behavior in your household.

More than one stepmom we interviewed noted that table manners were something they taught and enforced with the support of the children's father. In all cases, the kids' biological mom did not teach or emphasize manners, and it usually related to the fact that there was no regular family meal. Kids made a sandwich or grabbed some cereal for dinner because mom was usually busy. When they did sit down together on a weekend, it was elbows on the table and cell phones all around.

Kelly told us that her husband's two daughters would forget for the first day of the visit what they were supposed to do in their dad's house. It wasn't just table manners, although that was part of it. It was using a coaster under a cold drink, not putting dirty shoes on the couch, and other basics of civilized life. Their mom never enforced any of these standards, so their idea of "good" and "bad" behavior was really different depending on whose house they were in. Fortunately, the girls seemed to remember where they were by the first evening and they "reverted" to good behavior.

Marcia had a much more serious problem. She caught her drunk, sixteen-year-old stepson watering his marijuana plants. Her immediate response was to confiscate the plants and grab his car keys. But she didn't. Technically, since they lived in a state where marijuana was legal and he only had four plants, the only things he was guilty of were underage drinking and violating their house rules. She took a deep breath and called his dad, who was on a business trip. Her simple question was, "What shall we do?" and not "What shall I do?"

Financial boundaries

Money issues can tear a family apart and blended families tend to be more vulnerable because people outside the household are involved. Money boundaries relate primarily to child support as well as allowances and other issues of financial fairness.

Some of the basics of having a good working relationship with an ex are related to child support. The responsibility of supporting the child is mutual, but the boundary—this is your side of the responsibility and that is mine—is often decided by a third party. That boundary is movable, but it should only be movable in favor of the well-being of the child. In other words, if you have the money and you trust your ex, then it is appropriate to give more.

In addition, to support the blending process, one of the things that needs to happen is that all kids in the household feel there is financial fairness. From payment for chores to standard allowances to estate planning, all children in the household should be treated as equals. Crossing over the line to financial favoritism for a biological child, for example, is corrosive.

Behavioral boundaries

Two prime examples of behavioral boundaries are parent-stepparent solidarity and sibling-stepsibling interaction.

Creating a united front in front of ex-spouses/partners is vital. No ex should be able to move into the emotional space that belongs to you and your partner, or to intrude on the way you run your household. We've probably all seen movies, or known real circumstances, where an ex continues to be an influential presence in the former spouse's life. Just say no.

Regarding the second point, the following story probably says more about the deprivation of sibling connection than any other thing we can think of. Cindy was an adorable, petite fourteen-year-old girl when her parents divorced. Her dad quickly remarried and did not allow her to even meet her stepsiblings. She would visit on weekends when they were with their biological mom, so she never met them. She would see photos in the house and even stay in the room of one of the girls. But they were like ghosts, haunting her imagination and making her feel isolated. The experience made her feel more and more punished by her parents' divorce and estranged from her father. This pretty, tiny girl became morbidly obese within a year. She tattooed her inflating arms and got piercings on her eyebrows, nose, and tongue. She streaked her hair purple and began doing drugs. Her preppy biological parents both cut her out of their lives. To her, this was a matter of "What else is new?"

Now in therapy, she still wants to know who her two stepbrothers and stepsister are. She wants to know why her father doesn't think she's as good as they are.

Not allowing kids to connect and develop a subsystem wherein they support one another is a mistake. They are all going through a transition; they can probably help each other. This is not an interaction to be forced, but it's one that can be supported.

Trevor's son and stepdaughter are the same age. They have a lot of the same homework and social challenges. They talk about those things and they help each other get through them. That's a practical and emotional place where stepsiblings can go and all parents/stepparents have to allow it to happen.

ESTABLISHING EQUALITY WHERE THERE IS INEQUALITY

Even biological children can be different in terms of physical appearance, intellect, and behavior. When children in a single household are the offspring of different parents, that reality complicates the "inequality" even more. Actually, an objective person (translate: not one of the parents involved) would not even use the word "inequality." However, a biological parent might be quick to conclude how much smarter or prettier her daughter is as compared to the "step." That's just another way of saying what that parent sees as the stripped-down truth: "The kids are not equal. Mine's better."

Biological siblings will naturally have similarities that may be in contrast to stepsiblings. Value systems, approaches to social situations, spending money, the relatively importance of education—all of these may clash. The couple at the heart of the blend must ensure not to value one sibling or set of siblings and their behavior over the others.

Ironically, this challenge to the blending process may be the easiest of all to meet if the couple truly sees their relationship as the core of the blended family. If they do, then their biological children and stepchildren have equal status in the home. However, if it's "all about the kids," then inequalities will invariably creep into the dynamic. It can be gender specific, too, depending on how the couple allows it to sort out: The boy who's really talented with robotics gets money to go to MIT; the girl who's pretty who wants to go to college is told to "just get married."

Celebrate the differences while you celebrate your unity as a family of equals. Secure parenting will engender trust among all the children that they are all total participants in the blend.

We started this book with a look at *Modern Family*, which captures a lot of insecure attachment styles as well as healthy doses of secure attachments between couples and in parenting. Inequality between the grown, biological children of Jay Pritchett and preteen Manny creep in sometimes, as so concerns Jay's gay son about his relationship being considered "equal." And then there's Gloria, Jay's sexy young wife, whose secure relationship with Jay is often scrutinized and judged to be an "unequal partnership."

But in episode after episode, the "inequalities" in the extended family seem to get sorted out. In one, Jay's birthday provided an opportunity for nearly everyone to feel slighted and to complain, but ultimately to come together as a successfully blended family.

Jay could afford a lot of extravagant getaways, but he wanted only one thing for his birthday: a few hours fishing on the lake. With a dry fly pinned to his shirt, he headed off for what he thought was a quiet day.

In this episode called "The One that Got Away," everyone in Jay's blend had colorful ideas about how to celebrate his birthday. And everything imploded, which meant that Jay had a busy, noisy day instead of a quiet one with trout flopping into an eight-foot fishing boat. He got calls to pick up his own birthday cake and rescue his adult children from a tree house—just a sampling of what went wrong. While they were stuck in the tree house, his son and daughter wondered if their stepsibling Manny would get a third of Jay's substantial estate.

But as the family seemed determined to end the day around a dinner table with loving tributes and gifts damaged by bad planning, Jay realized Manny wasn't there. He walked out to their pool and saw him sitting in the little fishing boat, waiting for Jay to sit with him and just relax.

Everyone had tried hard—with good intentions—to celebrate Jay's birthday. Ultimately, it was Manny's "gift" that made it clear how sincere everyone in this blended family was about making Jay happy. All the thoughts about whose gift was better, who had the right outfit, and other slightly paranoid expressions of inequality dissolved. Theirs was an odd blend, but it worked.

POINTS TO CONSIDER

One of the people who graciously consented to talk to us for this book is a family therapist and colleague of Trevor's, Kathy Koslow. A veteran of blended families, she also wrote a paper about stepparenting when she was getting her master's degree. The three points she makes about the challenges to family counselors in helping blended families are a good summary of the underlying reasons why they have unique issues and opportunities. Here are the three points:

First, stepfamilies are created through loss. Divorce or death turns a first-marriage into a single-parent home and requires the family to adjust to many new realities. When the parent re-couples and a new family constellation is formed, the members must again adjust to major changes in their lives. While adults experience re-coupling as something positive in their life, children often see it as a loss.

Second, as opposed to first-marriages, remarriages form "instant families." As such, the adults have very little time to work on their relationship; they are immediately immersed in stepfamily life with its myriad difficulties and complexities. The difficulties and complexities often impinge on their relationship-building time and the time they do have together is often child-focused. Every member of the new family, however, must adjust to their "instant family": Parents now have stepchildren, children now have step siblings, and they all have an extended kin network—all of whom are strangers, but are expected to behave as though they are family.

Third, our society has not come up with an adequate way in which to language stepfamilies—stepparents are not the *biological* parents; the stepfamily is not the *natural* family or the *nuclear* family. The opposite of biological and natural are negative connotations, that is, unnatural and abnormal. Step relations have been negatively referenced throughout literature: "wicked stepmother," "evil stepfather," and "ugly step sister," to name a few. Indeed, it is difficult to find positive languaging or images of a family brought together through marriage, whether they are called stepfamilies, blended families, or bi-nuclear families.[3]

Blended families are borne out of trauma, whether it's divorce, death, or abandonment. For any normal person, pain and stress will be present and will show up in your body; this is not up for debate. In some cases, divorce may not appear on the surface to be traumatic to the adults going through it, but it is on some level. And it does represent trauma to children. Healing hurt feelings can take years, and may even take on the magnitude of full-blown post-traumatic stress syndrome (PTSD) symptoms. Being aware of your partner's—and your children's—stress and hurt is a critical first step in helping everyone heal. Being aware of how you and your partner physically manifest stress is a second critical step. Take both of them.

NOTES

1. Gwen Dewar, "Has natural selection wired your brain for baby talk?" *Parenting Science*; http://www.parentingscience.com/baby-communication.html.

2. Teresa Farroni, Enrica Menon, Silvia Rigato, and Mark H. Johnson, "The perception of facial expressions in newborns," *The European Journal of Developmental Psychology*, 4(1) (March 2007): 2–13; http://www.ncbi.nlm.nih.gov/pmc/articles/PMC2836746/

3. Kathryn Koslow, "Stepfamilies" (unpublished thesis), Fairfield University, Graduate School of Education and Allied Profession, Marriage and Family Therapy Department; accepted January 30, 2013.

Chapter 4

Stepparenting Issues with Preteens

Inside Out is the story of a harsh transition for an eleven-year-old girl named Riley. Uprooted from her Minnesota home, friends, and favorite sport—hockey—she is forced to move to San Francisco because of her father's new career venture. Fighting to hold her together emotionally, to protect her psyche and spirit, are the "stars" of the Pixar movie: Joy, Sadness, Disgust, Anger, and Fear.

If the movie were about an eleven-year-old moving into a new home with a blending family, the same emotional events might well have happened: some happy memories and imaginings were lost forever, and parts of her personality crumbled as she struggled to cope with challenges that seemed far too great for a child of her age.

Spoiler alert: Just as Joy kept Riley connected to her family in her early years, Sadness helped her reconnect during her difficult transition. Allowing her feelings of loss to surface aroused the empathy of her parents. Her vulnerability invited expressions of love as well as her parents' own displays of vulnerability. It's a vivid depiction of an important truth in both parenting and romantic relationships: The more fluent we are about our emotions, the more resilient we are in life.

Riley's "islands" of personality in the beginning of the story embodied the people and things that defined her as a child: family, goofball, friendships, honesty, and hockey. Goofball Island crumbled first.

Even when a child's life is stable, in moving toward puberty, silliness (symbolized by Goofball Island) is probably the first to go. There may be events like a divorce between parents, move to a new city, or death of someone close that would hasten the loss of silliness, but it's probably bound to happen anyway. A parent or stepparent might notice seriousness creeping in, or it might take shape suddenly. It's not the time to spotlight it through fussing or distract from it by entertaining. It's the time to pay attention to feelings about changes—changes in the child's circumstances, relationship, activities, and body.

Rapid changes in physical size and both mental and physical capabilities can bring on a great deal of confusion in the preteen age group, which we're roughly defining here as eight- to twelve-year-olds. In a blended household, differences in meals, environment, and maybe even a change of schools can amplify the confusion to the point where kids are distraught. A child's attachment to his or her biological parent—who may be the one obvious "constant" in the child's life—may make it extremely hard for the stepparent to forge a bond, enforce rules, and even seem like a welcome addition to life. Even when the bond with a stepparent seems solid, the preteen years can be a time of turmoil.

Following our discussion of the five top challenges related to stepparenting kids in the 8–12 age group, we offer a true story of how a blended family in Texas happened to meet all of them. We say "happened to" because some of the steps the biological father and stepmother took were planned, and some of them were natural outgrowths of their changing circumstances.

The five challenges we've identified are:

1. The growing need for autonomy
2. The continuing need to interact regularly with parental figures
3. The need to feel respected as almost-grown-up people, not "little kids"
4. The need for confidence-builders
5. The need for you to not be an embarrassment

THE GROWING NEED FOR AUTONOMY

Kids of this age have a natural desire to turn to their friends and pull away from parental figures, but there may be some special challenges facing stepparents. Kids may want to test their relationships with their stepparents by staying close to their biological parents and keeping a distance from their stepparents. Conversely, they might pull away from one or both biological parents and treat you more like a buddy. (So much depends on the dynamic of the household!) They may even threaten to run away—one way to exercise power over any parental figure.

It's important not to take it personally, unless you've been excessively punitive or demanding, for example. The withdrawal is not a rejection of you and/or your parenting partner as much as it is a normal lurching forward toward young adulthood. This is simply part of a social readjustment, so try to be tolerant of the change.

Preadolescent kids become increasingly more aware of how their peers see them and the importance of what those peers think of them often supersedes what parents think. Keep in mind that preadolescence seems to be ending sooner now than in previous generations due to various shifts in social, intellectual, and physical influences. According to the National Institutes of Health, the onset of puberty now typically occurs for girls between the ages of 8 and 13, and for boys between the ages of 9 and 14.[1]

Based on these studies, girls especially hit puberty at an earlier age than they used to and along with that come new attitudes, and preferences of how to spend time and with whom to spend it. You may feel as though the stepchild you met last year has transformed into a different person and that your presence in his life is somehow related to the emotional and psychological changes you've witnessed. Keep your eye on the physical changes as a reminder of what's actually happening. This isn't about you, but your response can help a preteen get through the transition.

To complicate matters, there are side effects of growth spurts and hormone production that can make a preteen need peer support and affirmation more than ever. Gawkiness, clumsiness, and the loss of perfect skin can cause kids of this age to be very self-conscious. Your reassurance that "you're fine" is hollow compared with a friend saying, "You look really great today. I saw Dana smiling at you!"

But for a preteen who has pulled away from her parents and stepparents and who is a victim of bullying, it can feel as though she has nowhere to turn. Bullying tends to take shape during this preteen period and, without friends to shore up the defenses, a kid can be left feeling extremely isolated. Therefore, even as you are respectful of the need for some autonomy, you need to have an open-door policy on communication and regular interaction with the preteen.

THE CONTINUING NEED TO INTERACT
REGULARLY WITH PARENTAL FIGURES

Psychotherapist Wendy Aronsson pointed to some very positive aspects of parent-child communication in her book *Refeathering the Empty Nest*. She cited the role that mobile technology has played in parents and kids staying in touch. With baby boomers and Generation X, it was a matter of finding a pay phone or going to a friend's house to make a call if they needed a ride home, for example. Now, it's a simple text: "Pls pick up at mall." The plus side of this is that parents and stepparents can communicate with a child without the message seeming like an intrusion. A casual "Need a ride?" text from stepmom is not nearly the same as paging a twelve-year-old girl in a shopping mall, with an intercom blasting out the message, "Mary Smith, please call home." How awful those broadcasts were for a kid in a small town at the local mall in 1985!

In contrast, there can be so much attention to the well-lit little screen that preteens neglect to make eye contact with parental figures. They don't actually see how much these adults care about them and want to communicate with them. They may be deprived of the meaningful interactions that can prevent them from feeling isolated from parents and alienated from the family as a whole.

Some of the stepparents we interviewed were adamant about maintaining the ritual of the family dinner to ensure parents and kids interacted daily. One stepmom even called eating a meal together "a portal to healthy communication." She noted that cell phones were not allowed at the table and that family members took turns offering topics for conversation. For a lot of families, this might be possible a couple of times a week, but work schedules, practices, and other demands on time make it unrealistic as a daily activity for a great many households.

Don't worry about it if yours is one of those households. There are other ways to support interaction between kids and parents and they can be as good as, or better, than meals together, according to Ann Meier and Kelly Musick from the University of Minnesota and Cornell University, respectively. Their study on the subject, published in the Journal of Marriage and Family, is called "Assessing Causality and Persistence in Associations between Family Dinners and Adolescent Well-Being." Their analysis sample was about 13,000 adolescents and they represented kids from homes with two biological parents, a stepparent in the home, a single parent, and grandparents or other adults serving as parental figures. The group included people of a variety of racial, ethnic, and socioeconomic backgrounds.

On the "pro" side of the meals-together debate, the researchers state:

> Children thrive on routine and stability, and meals are an important part of what organizes a child's daily activities. But more than just routine, mealtime may entail patterned, symbolic practices for many families, including favorite foods, structured roles, and expressions of gratitude. These rituals may be comforting, promoting feelings of closeness and belonging and providing a break from daily stressors. Family meals may thus afford a regular and positive context for parents to connect with children emotionally, to monitor their social and academic activities, and to convey values and expectations—mechanisms that may directly foster children's well-being.[2]

There are plenty of other activities involving shared parent-child time, however, they often lack the same potential for ritual and focus—unless you think about it and implant some elements that promote quality interaction. For example, maybe it's not feasible to have meals together every day, but at least one parent is available to help with homework, you go to movies together occasionally, and/or there is a morning ritual of talking about plans and hopes for the day while driving to school. One of the people we interviewed had parents who both did shift work, so weekday meals were eat-and-run, but every Saturday and Sunday, the family ate together. The other family ritual was going to church on Sunday and then just "hanging out in the kitchen."

The two professors who conducted the study examined three outcomes capturing well-being in the kids they studied: (a) depressive symptoms, (b) substance use, and (c) delinquency. Then they proceeded to try to assess whether or not the frequency of the adolescents' participation in family meals made it more or less likely that they would experience any or all of those three. They considered frequent family dinners five or more per week, with low being 0 to 2 and medium being 3 to 4.

They asked a few other critical questions, though, that helped them ascertain the quality of the relationships kids had with their parental figures. One of them was about activities they had done with a parent (or stepparent) in the previous four weeks: shopping, playing a sport, going to a religious service or event, attending the theater/movie or a museum, or working on a school project. Another important measure of the quality of the relationship relates to the previous point about an adolescent's growing need for autonomy. The researchers examined how much parental control was involved in their interactions. They also examined to what extent the kids could make their own decisions about curfew, friends, clothing, television, bedtime, and what they ate.

In conclusion, what emerged was that meals were often part of a happy family story, but there was a lot more going on that engendered healthy interaction between kids and parents.

> We looked at adolescents over the course of a year and examined how changes in the frequency of family dinners related to changes in well-being. If adolescents were eating family dinners more often a year later, were they better off? We found that following teenagers over a year provided even weaker evidence for the causal effects of family dinners on adolescent well-being—only the effect of family dinners on teen depressive symptoms held up. There was no effect on drug and alcohol use or delinquency.[3]

In short, eating together didn't necessarily cause better relationships; they might be better viewed as reinforcement of them. If kids talk about their lives with their parents at dinner, then there's a potentially fruitful experience at mealtime. But if they're simply watching the same TV program while they sit in the same room eating, then the "togetherness" is a little weaker unless they talk about the program later. The researchers concluded:

Family dinners may be part and parcel of a broader package of practices, routines, and rituals that reflect parenting beliefs and priorities. Interventions aimed at increasing the frequency of family meals may be successful only if they can change the family habits that tend to go along with eating as a family.[4]

Find ways to interact with your preteen that suit your family structure and dynamics. Aiming artificially for "interaction times" that have worked in other homes may be a detrimental approach. If you like to shop and your stepdaughter likes to shop, then go to the mall together. Discover more about each other's tastes and what you like about one store over another. There isn't anything inherently less valuable about spending an afternoon shopping together than having chicken in the same room at the same time.

THE NEED TO FEEL RESPECTED AS ALMOST-GROWN-UP PEOPLE, NOT "LITTLE KIDS"

Three types of activities can help preteens feel more respected as maturing people—but they will probably only want to deal with two of them! The three are chores, responsibilities, and life skills, with chores being the category of activity that they probably wish you would forget about.

Knowing that they have certain types of chores to do reminds them that you think of them as more grown up than little kids who aren't capable of doing much. They might hate them, but realizing you trust your twelve-year-old to rev up the lawn mower on her own and cut the grass is a chore that she knows you would not ask her seven-year-old brother to do. Chores aren't necessarily linked to life skills, but they are linked to life discipline.

Age-appropriate chores for a preteen would include keeping his bedroom clean, helping with laundry, taking out the recycling, making his own lunch, and washing the minivan periodically.

One stepmom we talked with asked her ten-year-old stepdaughter to do two things, and only two things, on a daily basis: empty the dishwasher and sweep the kitchen floor. Day after day, the stepmom would come from work and the stepdaughter would not have done either of the chores. So she went to the girl's biological father and said, "What am I supposed to do? I don't want to yell at her." He suggested offering her $10 a week to do the chores. So the stepmom tried that. That didn't work either. So, she said to her one day, "We are going to empty the dishwasher and sweep the floor together." The stepdaughter said, "Okay." They did it together, even as the stepmom explained what she had done that day at work; she had been basically on her feet most of the day in a customer service role at a store. Finally, it sunk in for the stepdaughter: "She's asking me to do these chores because she's exhausted.

They take ten minutes max. I'm such a jerk." They did the chores together a couple of more times and then she started doing the chores by herself—and, yes, she did get the $10.

Responsibilities are things that support the development of life skills. They would cover things like independently scheduling time for completion of homework. So, instead of treating your ten-year-old like a little kid and saying, "Sit down right now and do your homework," you shift the responsibility for knowing when to do it and scheduling ample time to do it to your child. That doesn't mean you should refuse to help if the child asks for some input; it just means you have backed off from being prescriptive about the process. Another example would be allowing kids to make their own decisions about what extracurricular activities to do and what to wear to school.

Some age-appropriate responsibilities have to do with personal standards, such as hygiene, and others relate to basic personal organization, such as keeping track of belongings like clothes and school notes. Others have to do with family needs, like babysitting a young sibling. These are not chores; these are important activities that affect the child's self-respect and ability to function, as well as the family's well-being.

Life skills are the things you teach your preteen that are big clues that you think she's growing up. They are things that then get put into practice so they aren't forgotten. Maintaining a bank account, creating a weekly schedule of duties and activities, and learning basic first aid are three things that kids in this age group can start to handle. These are skills they can learn from lots of sources, but to whatever extent they can learn them from you, it's one more opportunity for you to demonstrate personally that you see your child as moving toward young adulthood.

THE NEED FOR CONFIDENCE-BUILDERS

In the movie *Blended*, preteen Tyler is the joke of his Little League team. Before he even becomes Tyler's stepdad—he's just a "buddy" at this point— Adam Sandler's character, Jim, gives him pointers that dramatically improve his batting. Those tips kick in during a big game and Tyler goes from being a joke to a hero with the winning home run of the game. Tyler's dad, Mark, repeatedly breaks promises to his son about coming out to games, so one way Jim helps build Tyler's confidence is just by caring enough to show up. Jim even tries to defer to the biological father, but Mark is an avoidant parent who walks away from his kids.

It may not be prudent or appropriate for a stepparent to do what Jim did, but then again, it might be exactly what a kid needs. Whether it's sports, music, or some other activity that's important to the child, if the stepparent can make a legitimate contribution—and the child seeks that help—then he or she should step up.

There are also plenty of subtle ways to help build a preteen's confidence. "Just" showing up for a game can be a very big deal, for example.

Keeping in mind that this can be a time of physical changes and awkwardness, a young adolescent might want your help looking good, especially if you have a parental presence during the school week.

Donna had acne even into her early adult years and was sensitive to the fact that her twelve-year-old stepdaughter, Zoe, was starting to deal with breakouts. Her skin issues weren't horrible, but they were enough to make her ask to stay home from school some days on the premise she was sick. By the time Donna married Zoe's father, she had perfect skin because she'd found a product that worked; her stepdaughter had never seen a blemish on her face.

One day, Donna casually said, "I use this every day," and held up a bottle. "If you want to try to it, I'll leave my travel bottle in your bathroom." Zoe tried the product and noticed a difference in a one day. "Thanks, Donna! This is great stuff!" she told her.

"Glad it worked for you. I'll order some for you, too. In the meantime, just keep that other bottle." And then Donna pulled out an old photo of herself with blotchy skin and showed it to Zoe. Her stepdaughter was shocked: "Whoa! What a difference."

Donna's gesture was a little thing that wasn't a little thing to Zoe. She felt better about herself than she had since she was 11.

THE NEED FOR YOU TO NOT BE AN EMBARRASSMENT

Throughout the book, we have described how the different attachment styles manifest in parenting. Harvard psychologist Catherine Steiner-Adair, author of *The Big Disconnect: Protecting Childhood and Family Relationships in the Digital Age*, has a colorful way of describing how the insecure attachment styles give rise to behaviors that kids find totally embarrassing. These behaviors are worse than having a stepfather show up at school in mint green golf pants. The Child Mind Institute interviewed her for an article called "10 Tips for Parenting your Pre-teen," in which she says that these behaviors can be divided into three categories—"scary," "crazy," and "clueless."

- **The "scary" parent** is the overly harsh, judgmental parent who weighs in too intensely on other kids' behavior.
- **The "crazy" parent** is the mom or dad who overreacts to a bad situation. The crazy parent amplifies the drama, throwing fuel on the preadolescent's already hyperreactive flame.

- **The "clueless" parent** is the one who just ignores stuff. These parents might seem oblivious or unconcerned to kids.[5]

Both the private and the public aspect of all three behaviors serve as an embarrassment to kids. Listening to a parent spout something mean-spirited, ranting about a situation, or walking away from a problem that needs an adult solution are all behaviors that make a kid want to pretend that you belong to someone else's family.

Effectively tackling these five challenges involves the coordinated effort of both the biological parent and the stepparent, not to mention co-parenting with the other biological parent. In this true story, a biological parent (not the partner of the stepparent) removed herself from the picture, leaving the preteen in a state of sadness, anger, and fear—much like Riley in *Inside Out*, except that this preteen was suddenly without her main attachment figure.

Pregnant at 18, Mary Kay never adjusted to being a mother. She married her fiancé, Dan, whom she met during freshman year of college, when he was a senior. After graduation, he zoomed into a good-paying job doing public relations for a lobbying group while she stayed at home with their daughter, Rachel. Ten years later, with a desire to go back to college and "make something of myself," she resigned as Rachel's mom. She left without fanfare one morning, ostensibly headed for a class at the community college, and never looked back. Dan got full custody of Rachel and Mary Kay headed off to a new life.

With his preteen daughter at home every day and his job demanding an almost 24/7 commitment, he felt boxed in. He met a pretty, single, twenty-six-year-old woman named Pam at a rally for a political candidate they both supported and they began dating.

Pam and Rachel talked and laughed easily together almost immediately. They both loved to cook and go to the beach, and even though Pam liked having her girlfriends come along sometimes, she seemed to enjoy it when it was just the two of them. With Rachel's blessing, Pam and Dan married six months to the day after they met.

Rachel rarely heard from her mother—she got a birthday card and a Christmas gift—and never spoke to her. One day she called Pam "mom." Pam quickly thought about the relative wisdom of encouraging that since Rachel really didn't have a mom in her life, but instead she decided not to react to it. On her own, Rachel went back to calling her by her first name.

About a year into the marriage, with Rachel now 12, Pam found herself crying every day. The sweet little girl who liked to cook and go to the beach had turned into a moody, sniping beast. Dan gave her Pam a lot of reassurance that it wasn't her fault, but that didn't make things any better. They sought family counseling, which is something Pam says every blending family should probably do.

They made a conscious decision to give Rachel autonomy in the process. They asked her if she wanted to come along to the sessions: "We never made her do it. We just invited her. Most of the time, she came with us, but sometimes she didn't. It seemed to work well that she could make the choice."

As Rachel turned 13, the joy in her life returned: She now had a baby brother to care for. Dan and Pam included her in the birth experience, so she felt connected to Eric from the second he took his first breath. She doted on him. Pam figured she was ultrasensitive to the need for mothering because of what had happened to her. She let Rachel have a lot of responsibility with Eric; that seemed to go a long way to making her feel respected and to building her self-esteem.

Rachel was also proud of Pam. She had a strong feeling every day that Pam would never leave. And she didn't. When Rachel turned 21, she decided to start calling Pam "mom." By then, Pam figured it was okay.

POINTS TO CONSIDER

We began this chapter with a description of eleven-year-old Riley's emotions, the "stars" of *Inside Out*, and will move toward a close with some humorous insights from blogger Laughing Abi about tweens and their multiple personalities—each of which presents parenting challenges and relationship opportunities. Abi is a stay-at-home mom who observed that her eleven-year-old daughter was not one person, but rather seven:

1. The BFF Age: 35–40.
This woman goes with me to get manicures, chats over lattes at Starbucks (always my treat), and goes out of her way to listen to my problems and help in any way possible. The BFF doesn't come around very often but when she does you can hear the angels singing from above.

2. The Sweetheart Age: 6.
This is the sweetest, dearest little girl you will ever meet. She loves to snuggle and give kisses. She will climb up on the couch next to you on any given night just to tell you how much she loves you. She comes around even less than the BFF.

3. The Devil's Twin Age: Unknown.
This evil twin usually lurks around my house during late afternoon hours. She looks exactly like the BFF or the Sweetheart but when you speak to her burning acid shoots out of her mouth and does not stop until you flee the room, screaming profanities. Occasionally she rears her ugly head early in the morning so beware.

4. The Einstein/Miss Independent Age: 11–20.

This girl knows everything and can do everything herself. Everything. The easiest way to identify her is by her language. She only speaks two words, "I know."

5. The Mature One Age: 18–22.

This is a young woman who knows how to handle herself. She tackles every chore with maturity. She does things without being asked. She engages in conversation with adults in a way that makes you consider admitting you are her parent. Unfortunately, she does not come around very often.

6. The Baby Age: 3–5.

Often confused with the Drama Queen, this child believes every single, itty, bitty, teeny, weeny injury is a near-death experience. She once asked to go to the emergency room because she bent her hair.

7. The Drama Queen Age: 10–20.

This girl is very similar to the Baby. However, she does not need to be injured to believe the world is ending. She only needs to be breathing. No clean jeans to wear? End of world. Can't find her hairbrush? End of world. It's Tuesday and she wants it to be Wednesday? End of world. Please note, the Drama Queen can instantly transform into the Devil's Twin without any warning or notice.[6]

There may be some hyperbole in Abi's description, but there's probably more accuracy than exaggeration. The bodies, personalities, interests, and emotions of kids in the 8–12 age group are morphing steadily. When we interviewed Tracy, she had just seen *Inside Out* and said she cried loudly when Riley's imaginary friend faded. We were a little surprised, since it was a moment any viewer could have seen coming. She explained that, when she married John, his son Nick was 8. His "best friend" was Scooter, who didn't have an age and about whom no one was even clear what specie "he" was. Scooter lived by a lake and the two of them would take walks together and throw rocks into the lake to scare the fish. About a year later, John, Tracy, and Nick moved from North Carolina to Northern California. Tracy asked Nick if Scooter had moved with them. "No! Duh! He wanted to stay in North Carolina." No one mentioned Scooter again for at least a year, when Tracy asked innocently if Nick had heard from Scooter. Nick rolled his eyes as if she'd lost her mind.

Trevor's daughter Olivia had a very grown-up realization when she was 11: Her half-sister was her whole sister. Here is her essay about what happened:

I sat on the ramshackle porch, gazing at the sun as it melted into the waves. The wicker chair hurt my sunburned back, and my brothers were still arguing over who had won the boogie boarding contest.

Michelle opened the creaky door behind me, and stood for a moment,
hand on her hip, regarding my weary look. "Come on, Olivia,"
she said, dangling the car keys. "Let's go for a drive."
I was ten; she was eighteen. She was the coolest person in the whole world.
That summer, she and I had built rituals around the simplest of tasks,
savoring trips to the grocery store, getting purposely lost on the windy
roads leading home, and making cookie dough just to eat it raw.
Spending so much time together was rare and delicious to us.
According to Einstein's theory of general relativity, gravity is a geometric
property of space and time. But it has emotional contours, too; the way one
is anchored in a family, for instance, a unit whose location and headcount
can change rapidly and without warning. My childhood was characterized
by random shifts in seemingly immutable properties, and the knowledge of
distance. When I was five, my dad moved our family across the country to
Connecticut, leaving Michelle behind. She was from his previous marriage,
and I was the product of his new one. Language became increasingly tricky,
especially later, after Dad divorced my mom, and moved on to yet another
family. After that, whenever I would try and explain my relationship to
Michelle, I still referred to her as my sister. I'd always wanted a sister.
"But she doesn't live with you," my classmates would respond, looking puzzled
By the time we arrived at the dilapidated cottage that summer, I
had begrudgingly begun using the prefix "half-" when regaling
outsiders with stories, if only to make sense. At the time, using the
word "half" still felt new to me, and a little like betrayal.
As the salty air whipped through the windows of Michelle's
car that afternoon, a question pounded in my chest.
"Do you feel like we're half-sisters?" I asked quietly and casually, like her
answer didn't matter, even though it did. With our father, we were days
on a calendar, a frequency of court-mandated time that ran perpendicular
to his life with his new family. Partial custody. *Half Sisters. My feelings*
for Michelle were the opposite of measured, they were huge, unbounded,
and I wanted my relationship with her to exceed easy fractions.
"Well, it's true," she said gently. "But 'half' makes it all about him, doesn't it? I
mean, Dad might have been how we met. He catalyzed our introduction and our
separation. But I think we've built our own unique thing without him. Don't you?"
She raised an eyebrow at me. "If you say 'no' I'm gonna die of heartache, Livvie."
I smiled so hard I thought my face would crack, and nodded fast instead of
answering. I didn't have the vocabulary for it yet, but she had just described
the force that bonded us, and I was grateful. Michelle has taught me so
much as I've grown, but this was the most important lesson: when you love
someone, space and time can't keep you apart. It is trust that will bring
you together, the gravitational pull that creates a home and a family. As
a child from a blended family transitioning into adulthood, I believe your
life is only as meaningful as the quality of the relationships you choose. I
have seen how poor relationships disintegrate and strong ones can defy all

odds, and as I discover the type of person I hope to be, I know one thing
for certain: circumstance won't define my relationships, integrity will.
"Let's not say 'half' anymore," I decided after a pause. "It's not how I feel."
"Deal," my sister said, and we drove on.

NOTES

1. "Puberty and Precocious Puberty: Overview," National Institutes of Health, Eunice Kennedy Shriver National Institute of Child Health and Human Development; https://www.nichd.nih.gov/health/topics/puberty/Pages/default.aspx.

2. Kelly Musick and Ann Meier, "Assessing Causality and Persistence in Associations Between Family Dinners and Adolescent Well-Being," *Journal of Marriage and Family* 74 (June 2012): 476–493, DOI: 10.1111/j.1741-3737.2012.00973.x, p. 477.

3. Ann Meier and Kelly Musick, "Is the Family Dinner Overrated," *The New York Times*, June 29, 2013; http://www.nytimes.com/2012/07/01/opinion/sunday/is-the-family-dinner-overrated.html?_r=2&hpw.

4. Ibid., Music and Meier, p. 492.

5. Juliann Garey, "10 Tips for Parenting Your Pre-teen," Child Mind Institute; http://www.childmind.org/en/posts/articles/2014-7-29-ten-tips-parenting-your-pre-teen.

6. http://www.scarymommy.com/articles/multiple-personalities?section=surviving-the-tween-years&u=gySFjpBZfX.

Chapter 5

Stepparenting Issues with Teens—Risk and Reward

Suddenly stepparenting a teenager, even if you have younger biological children of your own, will be a shock to the system unless you've taught in junior high or high school. There are many misconceptions about why adolescents do some of the outrageous things they're known for. It's not "just hormones." It's not just "the rebellious years." Their amazing—and in many ways, adult—brains are giving them certain signals that can support healthy, productive risk-taking in the future. It's what author Jim McCormick, founder of the Research Institute for Risk Intelligence, calls "intelligent risk-taking." He cautions that a teen's developing brain isn't quite ready to take on risk in a way that makes it a powerful tool, as it could be for an entrepreneur, for example. But the impulse to take risks is inherently good and, as a parent, you can help shape a young person's risk profile so that when his cognitive brain catches up with the rest of him, he won't have the life squeezed out of his risk-taking impulses.[1] It's important to remember that risk-taking does have a positive side borne out of thoughtful evaluation of risk and reward—we wouldn't have democracies or free-market economies if it weren't for risk-takers. In fact, we wouldn't have survived as a species unless we figured out how to take intelligent risks. So the good news for you is that the teenager's drive to take risks can *add* a lot to your family happiness and dynamics if you help him channel it; it can be the source of good feelings, adventures, and positive outcomes (despite some bumpiness along the way). But when you're dealing with someone roughly between 11 and 21, risk-taking can come with a downside: *They see the rewards of risk as more compelling than the consequences.*

The sense of reward from risk actually causes their oxytocin production to spike; oxytocin is the same hormone that is produced during lovemaking and giving birth, so it's a powerful feel-good chemical. (There is more about

65

oxytocin in the discussion of trust as one of The Five Things You Need to Succeed.)

Part of your success in parenting, therefore, is knowing how that reality of risk-taking plays out specifically in your child/stepchild's life. First of all, there are different types of risks: physical, social, intellectual, creative, relationship, emotional, and spiritual. They can all make those years of adolescence and young adulthood both difficult and fulfilling. In his book, *The Power of Risk*, McCormick gives basic definitions of the categories of risk named above[2]; we've just added notes, examples, and stories about how the type of risk might manifest itself in the teenage years:

PHYSICAL

These are activities that involve the possibility of injury. The most significant one for teens is driving a car, although sports figure prominently too. And, depending on where you live, there could be substantial physical risks in riding public transportation.

A key point is that it shouldn't be viewed as only a physical risk; the physical risk is compounded by the social aspect of driving with friends, playing sports in front of a crowd, or taking a subway to meet a friend in another borough of New York, for example.

Boys are more inclined to physical risks than girls if the context is a gym or ball field, but if sex is put into the category of physical risk, then girls are just as willing to "go for it" as boys in many cases. You want to make sure, without scaring the life out of your teen, that he understands the worst-case scenarios of physical risk-taking. At the same time, it's important to back off and let him decide to do something or not to do it if it's an age-appropriate choice. This can be a really tough call for a parent, and even more complicated if the adult who wants to intercede is a concerned stepparent. What if your teen faced a decision like Connor Sheehan, for example?

Sheehan played football for Harvard. When he did an interview with the "official website of Harvard athletics," he was asked the question, "How has playing football at Harvard better prepared you for life?" His reply: "Playing football, I have learned how to deal with adversity."[3] There's a backstory on Connor that brings this comment to life. When he was at Anderson High School in Austin, Texas, he was a running back and cocaptain of the football team, the Trojans. A sprained ankle had kept him in rehab for weeks. He faced a choice: continue to nurse his ankle and miss playing in the school's first-ever playoff, or risk a complicating injury. He decided to play. The Trojans won. He reinjured his ankle, and then went on to play for Harvard.

He knew the potential consequences, accepted them in light of the potential reward, and made up his mind to "deal with adversity."[4]

No one could blame a parent for wanting to err on the side of caution, but knowing when not to force caution on a teen is vitally important. Lauren's mom was on a plane headed to a business meeting in Australia when the fifteen-year-old asked her stepdad, Tom, if she could go with her best friend to do bungee jumping. Her friend's mom was going to do it with them. Tom knew he couldn't reach Lauren's mother for hours and the girls wanted to go that afternoon. He went to the website of the bungee jumping company and said to his stepdaughter, "This looks like fun." He was inclined to let her go, but he remembered that Lauren's mom had a college friend die during a skydiving accident. Even though this was a lot different, he was concerned that she wouldn't approve. He told her to text her dad and get his permission. The dad was in a meeting and just sent her a quick reply: "If your mom and Tom are okay with it, then go."

Tom felt like he was in a real bind. He explained his quandary to Lauren, who had a very grown up solution: "Why don't you come with us, Tom? You said it looked like fun." So he did. Lauren's mom later made it clear that if he hadn't gone, she would have been very upset. But the way it worked out was fine with her.

Other thoughts on physical risk-mitigation mostly fall into the discussion of the next category—social risks.

SOCIAL

Risks such as introducing yourself to someone you don't know or putting yourself in an unfamiliar social situation, where there exists the possibility of embarrassment, are examples of social risks. For a teen, it might be going to a party hosted by someone from a "different group" from the one she usually associates with.

Choice of clothes or places to hang out involves that all important "peer review" as much as behavior associated with a physical risk; wearing last year's jeans or hanging out at the gym could be viewed as social risks, depending on what the peers are doing.

But unlike physical risks which are made riskier by a social component and which therefore you might want to help mitigate—"You can drive to the game, but you may only have one friend in the car at a time"—many social risks are probably none of your business, unless they involve keeping company with kids using alcohol or drugs, or encouraging other behavior that could damage the child for life. Choosing what jeans to wear is an age-appropriate decision and you're wise to step back from as many of those as you can. If your stepdaughter asks you how she looks in them, or whether another pair of jeans might be better, then say something. Otherwise, you're probably just interfering. Social risks teach valuable life lessons.

Teens can go to extremes, of course, when it comes to something simple like choosing a pair of jeans. When Susan's fourteen-year-old-stepdaughter, Jen, decided to leave for school one morning in what appeared to be a pair of high-cut Daisy Dukes, she gave her a firm, "Come here, young lady. You are not going to school in shorts with your butt cheeks hanging out."

"Yes, I am," she snapped as she picked up her backpack and headed to the door. "Mike! Please come here." She wanted the girl's father to see what was going on. When he came into the room, he couldn't figure out what the problem was. "Mike, she's planning to go to school in those shorts!"

Mike calmly said, "That's what she wants to go to school in and if she shouldn't be going to school in them, then it's up to the principal to send her home to change." Susan couldn't believe her ears, but she did not want to disagree with Mike in front of his daughter, so she shrugged her shoulders and left the room.

Jen learned the hard way that she had taken a social risk that wasn't worth taking. As soon as she got to school, boys and girls made vulgar comments about the outfit. She left after her first class and came back home to change. The Daisy Dukes went into the trash.

INTELLECTUAL

Risks such as taking a tough course in school or joining a science or language club are "public" intellectual risks. Reading *War and Peace* or *A Brief History of Time* is essentially a private activity and so the risk isn't necessarily complicated by social pressures or expectations. Teens sometimes take public intellectual risks to gain points with peers or to arouse attention from someone in whom they have a sexual interest. In the case of the latter, the teen has created a combination of a social and intellectual risk, or a relationship and intellectual risk. In the former case, she might be driven purely by intellectual curiosity.

Seeing that your teen is taking an intellectual risk provides an opportunity to ask questions that might lead to an actual conversation with her. In fact, if you've never read *A Brief History of Time*, this might be a good time to get on the same page as her.

CREATIVE

Risks such as painting, taking on a writing challenge, or performing all put some level of talent up for evaluation. Trying out for the school play would be the kind of creative risk a teen might take. Again, this might be compounded by the desire to be in the play because friends or a girlfriend/boyfriend is involved.

A teen can suddenly become extremely vulnerable in the process of creative risk-taking. When potter and home furnishings designer Jonathan Adler was at the Rhode Island School of Design, his pottery teacher told him he was horrible and should study law instead.[5] He persevered and now has a global empire of 26 home furnishing stores that carry his name. But what if something comparable happened to your teenager over a painting, a recital, or a poetry reading? It could be devastating. Again, he's making age-appropriate choices that can engender valuable life lessons, but watch out for extreme highs and lows in creative risk-taking.

RELATIONSHIP

Risks such as a willingness to pursue a new love relationship, spend time with someone despite an uncertain outcome, or make a relationship commitment are in this category. For a teen, dating—or just "hanging out" with—someone in whom he has a sexual interest means the possibility of heartbreaking rejection.

Psychologist and author Nancy Kalish (*Lost & Found Lovers*) cautions parents not to belittle a teen relationship by calling it "puppy love" or dismiss a rejection as forgettable and insignificant.

> Parents question the ability of teenagers to know what love is, yet they accept their teenagers' statements, "I love you, Mom and Dad," with full appreciation and at face value. If adults accept that teenagers can love parents truly, then shouldn't they also accept that teen romances are "real" love?
>
> Adults who underestimate the strength of the bond—or the impact of the loss—of a first love may have forgotten what a blow it was when they lost their own first loves. They may even try to comfort teenagers with lighthearted lessons: a surprising number of men and women wrote to me to bitterly complain about parents who joked years ago, "Don't worry! Boyfriends/girlfriends are like buses . . . a new one comes along every ten minutes!" This was not helpful, and it was not funny. The loss of a first love can be so crushing to some teenagers that they become suicidal.[6]

Kalish reinforces her point with the result of a survey she conducted of 1,600 people whom she asked how they felt about reuniting with a first love. The respondents were between 18 and 92 years of age. She found that 56 percent of the participants said they would not want to go back to that first love, 19 percent weren't sure, and 25 percent said they would. She then makes a point that parents of teens are wise to keep in mind: "Even the adults who had no current interest in their first loves, including those who had only bitter memories, revealed that these early romances influenced their lifelong attitudes about love, and even about themselves."[7]

EMOTIONAL

This category involves risks that require a personal to be emotionally vulnerable, so there is some overlap with relationships. But our intent is to differentiate between romantic/sexual love and other types of emotional involvement.

Out of all the types of risks listed here, this is the one that *must* occur in order for the members of the new family to come together in harmony. It's the one that a parent and stepparent need to encourage the kids, and each other, to take even though the possibility exists that rejection or other emotional pain can occur. In a blended family, there are bound to be tons of emotional risks associated with new siblings, a new parent figure, new grandparents, and so on. So, in addition to the teen going through the usual relationship risks involving some kind of sexual interest, this young person is also forced by circumstances to take different kinds of relationship risks at home as well. That's a lot of emotion-focused risk-taking for someone still in junior high or high school!

In the previous chapter, we introduced the story of Rachel and her stepmother, Pam. Rachel's abandonment by her biological mother made her extremely vulnerable; she always had her dad, but the woman who was her primary attachment figure for ten years had suddenly disappeared from her life. Pam couldn't think of a single, particularly memorable, moment when Rachel took an emotional risk; she saw every expression of trust, love, and need as an emotional risk. Even during the most troubled times, when she made the choice to join her father and stepmother in therapy sessions, Rachel was very vulnerable. She had no previous experience of counseling and didn't know what she might be in for. The level of trust she put in her dad and this nice woman he married gave everyone hope that they could be a family.

Of course, even when everyone takes the emotional risks that are required to make the blend come together, a rule of thumb is that it takes many families about seven years to achieve what The Brady Bunch achieved in about 27 minutes.

SPIRITUAL

This relates to the willingness to place trust in concepts that aren't supported by tangible or visible evidence, or which a person doesn't fully understand. You might want your teen to take spiritual risks, but preaching won't be nearly as effective as leading by example.

One of the notable success stories of a blended family in Hollywood is the merger of director Steven Spielberg and actor Kate Capeshaw, whom Spielberg met when he cast her in *Indiana Jones and the Temple of Doom*. Married in 1991, their combined households, along with adoptions and births, ultimately made them a family of nine. When they married, their merged households included children who were 15, 6, 3, and 1, and then they added two birth children and an adopted daughter within the next five years.

There are things to be learned from the relationship—one of the factors contributing to family unity is Capeshaw's choice to commit to her husband's religion; this was not something he asked her to do, but something she wanted to do. Her becoming Jewish and giving all of the children a Jewish upbringing is something Spielberg acknowledges as a family asset.

Research conducted on teen risk-taking can help you see how you and your child/stepchild are different in your decision-making. Specifically, it illuminates the roles of reward and consequences in both teenaged and adult risk-taking.

Laurence Steinberg at Temple University in Philadelphia is a developmental psychologist specializing in adolescence. The prime time for risk-taking is around the age of 15, and his assessment of the fourteen- to seventeen-year-olds, who are precisely in that key range, is that they can reason their way through many challenges just as well as adults.[8] However, he has found a big difference in the way they *respond* to challenges that reveals a great deal about the unique behavior of adolescence—and it all has to do with their perception of reward.

Steinberg describes a video game study that involved adolescents (mean age 14), youths (mean age 20), and adults (mean age 34) in his paper, "A Social Neuroscience Perspective on Adolescent Risk-Taking." The tests involved playing a computer driving game under one of two conditions. The participants were either alone during the test or they were being watched by two friends of their age group. In one scenario, the game showed a car approaching an intersection. The participant would see the light turn yellow, and then would have to decide whether to brake or to try to make it through the intersection before a wall appeared, resulting in the car crashing into it (much more dramatic than a red light). The longer the person could drive without stopping, the more points he or she would earn.

When subjects were alone, levels of risky driving were comparable across the three age groups. However, the presence of friends doubled risk-taking among the adolescents, increased it by fifty percent among the youths, but had no effect on the adults, a pattern that was identical among both males and females . . . The presence of peers also increased individuals' stated willingness to behave in an antisocial fashion significantly more among younger than older subjects, again, among both males and females.[9]

Steinberg concluded, therefore, that it isn't that young people don't have the brains to figure out what's the "sensible" thing to do, but rather, that their much higher regard for reward compels them to take bigger risks. The social reward of having peers admire their "guts" is an unbelievable high.

Now consider the downside. When someone in this age group experiences social rejection, the pain is as intense—or more intense—than the pleasure of acceptance and accolade. As we wrote previously in *Forging Healthy Connections*, brain-scan studies indicate that the connection we feel to other human beings plays a key role in the biochemical activity that either supports good health or weakens it. In the case of adolescents, you might say metaphorically that the lights are brighter and the sounds are louder in this "movie" of how connectivity affects physical and mental health. As author David Dobbs indicated in his cover article for *National Geographic* on the new science of the teenage brain:

> Knowing this might make it easier to abide the hysteria of a 13-year-old deceived by a friend or the gloom of a 15-year-old not invited to a party. These people! we lament. They react to social ups and downs as if their fates depended upon them! They're right. They do.[10]

The changes in the brains of humans—from adolescence to young adulthood—are the reason why some of the responses and decisions of adolescents and young adults seem inexplicable—not just to adults, but also to their younger siblings. A teen has already gone through a lot of brain development related to emotion, but the portion that still has not matured is the prefrontal cortex. It is responsible for critical abilities enabling intelligent risk-taking, namely, planning ahead, impulse control, understanding the consequences of actions, and the appropriateness of one's behavior.

Robert Hedaya, clinical professor of psychiatry at the Georgetown University, explains the development process with the metaphor of interstate highways and secondary and tertiary roads. First of all, there are lots of these highways and roads and they lead to points of convergence; in the brain, these points are the nuclei. One of the major "hubs" is the amygdala, which controls "rage, fear, and sex. It also tells us (before we are consciously aware) whether a situation is safe, exciting, or dangerous, and our body reacts (again, before we are aware) immediately to this unconscious reflex."[11] Feeding into the amygdala are connections from the prefrontal cortex. So if the amygdala screams, "That dude's dangerous—I should break his jaw!" it's the signals from the prefrontal cortex that helps a person exercise control and, perhaps, plan a different course of action. Without a fully developed prefrontal cortex, of course, the teen is at a disadvantage in terms of quickly formulating that alternative response.

While this brain development is occurring, the teen is also losing her mind—part of it, anyway. The process is called "pruning" and means that certain interests, and even skills, will disappear if they are not sustained through practice that "grooves" the brain. Hedaya explains:

> During the teen years, under the influence of massive new hormonal messages, as well as current needs and experiences, the teenager's brain is being reshaped, and reconstructed. Information highways are being speeded up (myelination), and some old routes, closed down (pruning); some are re-routed and reconnected to other destinations. And above all, old information highways are making lots of new connections to other highways, and other cities and towns (sprouting). It's a massive construction project, unlike anything that occurs at any other time in life. In such a situation, things rarely flow smoothly, and surprise destinations thrive. This reconstruction explains why the personality and stability that was evident just a year or two before adolescence recedes, and suddenly new perspectives, and reactions abound.
>
> One of the important things to remember is that what a teen does and is exposed to during this critical time in life, has a large influence on the teen's future, because experience and current needs shape the pruning and sprouting process in the brain. So if a teen is playing lots of video games, this will shape the brain in such a way that they might become an excellent fighter pilot, but becoming an accountant or researcher will be less possible. . . . Being exposed to drugs, computer sex, or violent movies, will also shape the brain and future of the adolescent, laying down the seeds of addiction and interpersonal conflict.[12]

With all of this significant change going on—not to mention growth spurts and hormonal shifts—it's no wonder that you are faced with a person who is changing on a daily basis. This is a person trying to clarify her identity and identify her values. In the process of taking all of the normal types of risks associated with junior high and high school, that identity and those values *will* be affected by peers; they also *need to be* affected by those in a parental, teaching, or mentoring role. You're providing practical assistance during the adventure. And like a trek up Mt. Everest with a professional guide, the adventure is still fraught with potential dangers, but your involvement is a necessary and rational element.

What we ask you to understand and embrace is that the teen's craving for risk-taking and its potential rewards should not be muted, ignored, dismissed, or mocked. Megan McArdle, author of *The Up Side of Down: Why Failing Well Is the Key to Success*, had an encounter with a teenager while on her book tour that set off a red alert for her:

> A high school girl approached me and explained that while daring greatly and failing occasionally might be splendid in theory, she couldn't possibly afford to take any risks, because she was in an International Baccalaureate program

where 4.0 GPAs were few and far between. This girl was 15. If you can't afford a single mistake at the age of 15, just when will be the right time to take some risks? When you're shopping for headstones? . . .

But we can't only blame the parents. Parents are hovering to cope with their own fears, such as the (completely false) sense they get from our modern news blizzard that the world is an extremely dangerous place for children. And because of their fear of the current economy—with the ever-higher educational hurdles that we've placed between high school graduates and stable, well-paying jobs—they simply can't afford to give their kids the freedom to fail, even if hovering comes at the cost of building psychological strength and character.[13]

Ultimately, the traits of adolescence and young adulthood need to be seen as important signs of the adaptability of our species. These are developmental steps that occur in adolescents throughout the world—in tribes and in cities—because they are part of a human being getting ready to grow up and move out. As in, move out of your house.

With this last statement in mind, consider to what extent the culture of your community and your family determine whether or not the teenage years actually do culminate in your young person moving out of the house. Culture shapes next steps, regardless of the continued urges for risk and reward. More and more, you see financial constraints—or simple desire for creature comforts—contributing to the decision of young people to stay at their parents' home, or come back home later, rather than create a home of their own.

Psychotherapist Wendy Aronsson, author of *Refeathering the Empty Nest*, tells a funny (unless you're the parents!) story of a young adult moving back home because he couldn't afford living on his own in Boston after college. It's the mother's lament of a basement full of her son's stuff and her thinking, "I wanted it to have an expiration date."[14] While this is a common story, it doesn't mean that the twenty-year-old came back home and either reverted to early childhood behavior or suddenly behaved like an adult. No. The same risk-reward impulses that applied in high school and at the college dormitory are still there, at least to some degree. But now he's back living in your house, so you get to experience the impulses with a refreshed perspective.

POINTS TO CONSIDER

Stepparenting a teenager involves some significant emotional risk-taking on your part—and you hope there is a reward waiting you! When you take an emotional risk with your teen, you inspire him to do the same. Everyone nurtures the blend when the parent and stepparent demonstrate capacity for love and friendship with each other and with the kids in the household. Everyone needs to know it's not just okay, it's vital, that people show they care about each other. It's the kind of risk-taking that goes a long way to helping to heal the trauma that is the inciting incident for the blend.

As for the other types of risks—the ones that are potentially life-threatening, for example—well-placed reminders that the risk equation involves consequences as well as rewards is a good idea.

Laurence Steinberg, the Temple University scientist referenced earlier in this chapter, emphasizes that teens have volcanic "pleasure centers." It the job of parents to understand, direct, and appreciate the phenomenon:

Nothing—whether it's being with your friends, having sex, licking an ice-cream cone, zipping along in a convertible on a warm summer evening, hearing your favorite music—will ever feel as good as it did when you were a teenager.[15]

NOTES

1. From an interview with Jim McCormick, June 4, 2015.

2. Jim McCormick, *The Power of Risk*, Maxwell Press, 2008, pp. 153–159.

3. "Football Q&A—Connor Sheehan," Official Website of Harvard Athletics, November 9, 2014; http://gocrimson.com/sports/fball/2014-15/releases/201410 30lqjj7y.

4. David Dobbs, "Beautiful Brains," *National Geographic*, October 2011, p. 38.

5. Interview with Jonathan Adler, "Wait, Wait . . . Don't Tell Me!" National Public Radio, May 2, 2015; http://www.npr.org/2015/05/02/403496085/not my-job-designer-jonathan-adler-gets-quizzed-on-new-coke.

6. Nancy Kalish, "Teenagers in Love," *Psychology Today*, June 2, 2009, revised 2013; https://www.psychologytoday.com/blog/sticky-bonds/200906/teenagers-in-love.

7. Ibid.

8. Ibid., Dobbs, p. 54.

9. Laurence Steinberg, "A Social Neuroscience Perspective on Adolescent Risk-Taking," Developmental Review, 2008 March; 28(1); 78–106; doi: 10.1016/j.dr.2007.08.002; http://www.ncbi.nlm.nih.gov/pmc/articles/PMC2396566/

10. Ibid., Dobbs, p. 55.

11. Robert J. Kedaya, "The Teenager's Brain," *Psychology Today*, June 3, 2010; https://www.psychologytoday.com/blog/health-matters/201006/the-teenagers-brain.

12. Ibid.

13. Megan McArdle, "Helicopter parents and the kids who can't," *The Denver Post*, July 12, 2015, 1D and 6D.

14. Wendy Aronsson, Refeathering the Empty Nest: Life After the Children Leave, Rowman & Littlefield, 2014, p. 135.

15. Laurence Steinberg as quoted by Elizabeth Kolbert, "The Terrible Teens," *The New Yorker*, August 31, 2015; http://www.newyorker.com/magazine/2015/08/31/the-terrible-teens.

Part II

THE FIVE THINGS YOU MUST HAVE TO SUCCEED

In our journey to give you the most practical, clear advice on what supports a sustainable "blend," we concluded there are five key elements. They are factors that surfaced time and again in our interviews, surveys, and research. The five are:

trust
vulnerability
empathy
truthfulness
structure

In the chapters in this section of the book, each of these elements receives separate focus, but the topics do intertwine and build on one another.

We realize you might look at this list and think that "structure" seems out of place with a list of behaviors that relate to connectedness. You might think, "All the other factors are about ways to improve closeness; structure sounds mechanical."

Here's the logic: There is movement in this list from emotion and feeling to cognition and decision-making. Of course you have to have structure all along the way as your family evolves, but you want those decisions to be informed by the feelings and emotional issues that are unique to your family. If you have lots of rules and expectations, for example, but they don't emerge from the context of empathetic interaction, then children are cheated. As neuroanatomist and author Jill Bolte Taylor quite correctly points out, "We are feeling creatures who think,"[1] so there is an essential and dynamic interplay between emotion and cognition that enables us to make the best choices in our relationships. Structure is critical to the success of your intimate love relationship as well as your parenting and stepparenting. But it needs to reflect how, and how well, you connect with those other people in your life.

Sometimes, regardless of the levels of intent and optimism, a blend does not happen or cannot be sustained because the connection isn't resilient. The couple may have love and enjoyment of each other, but the people in the household never become part of a cohesive whole. They never become a family.

Blends that work see love as expansive; it's felt by everyone in the fold, all of whom feel safe with each other. They know what trust, vulnerability, empathy, and truthfulness feel like, even though they may have to work at them.

And then in contrast, there are "families" like the one that formed when Tim and Dawn got together.

Tim married Dawn three years ago, when he was 40 and she was 47. She brought two girls to the marriage, ages 13 and 9. A perennial bachelor, Tim had no intention of trying to parent the girls; he figured they already had a father who lived two miles away and he could see them often. He also did not like his own stepfather. Somewhere in the recesses of his consciousness he thought that stepparenting was an innately flawed concept. His attitude has been, "If the kids aren't yours by birth, stay out of the way."

Dawn made an assumption that Tim would change as he got to know them and they built a home together. His habits and attitudes are deeply ingrained, though. When he makes a sandwich for lunch, even if the girls are in the kitchen with him, he generally doesn't offer to make anything for them. It isn't as though he doesn't like them; they just aren't on his radar—unless they do something to annoy him.

In the first year of Dawn and Tim living together, if Dawn's daughters did something Tim didn't like, he would blurt out an order, "Don't do that; do this." In an attempt to coordinate with Tim on these outbursts of discipline, Dawn said, "When I call you 'honey' that means you need to step back and talk to me about how you're communicating with my daughters . . . and I don't mean talk to me in front of them."

That has ended up working fairly well, but Tim has never really connected with the girls. They are growing up under the same roof, but there is no blend.

The girls are not part of a blend in their father's home either. The woman he married gives her biological son everything he wants, but puts strict limits on what the girls can do, where they can go, and even what they eat at the house. They are tired of the rules and have asked if they can stop visiting on a regular basis. They feel close to their mom, and see her as their only parent.

In both cases, the parents seem to have stable, happy marriages to their second spouse. It can't be said, therefore, that they made bad choices, even though their choices have not lead to blended families. The unfortunate victims of the choices are, of course, the two girls. They have a loving, devoted mom, an absentee father, an unpleasant stepmother, and mom's nice husband who basically ignores them.

This is what a home looks like that lacks connection among all the people in it. Can they "fix" it? Possibly. If they were to take the messages in the upcoming chapters to heart, maybe they would see what they're missing.

NOTE

1. Jill Bolte Taylor, "The Neuroanatomical Transformation of the Teenage Brain"; https://www.youtube.com/watch?v=PzT_SBl31-s

Chapter 6

Trust and Trustworthiness

Trust is the foundation of all securely attached relationships.

Conductor Charles Hazelwood vividly describes how he can't do his job well without trust—anymore that you can function well as a partner or parent without trust.

> I have to trust the orchestra, and, even more crucially, I have to trust myself. Think about it: when you're in a position of not trusting, what do you do? You overcompensate. And in my game, that means you over-gesticulate. You end up like some kind of rabid windmill. And the bigger your gesture gets, the more ill-defined, blurry and, frankly, useless it is to the orchestra.[1]

The downward spiral from shaky trust to overcompensation to desperate acts puts fragile relationships in great jeopardy. As with an orchestra that lacks a solid, trusting relationship with their conductor, the music suffers. Everyone who hears it knows that it isn't quite right, even if they aren't aware of it on a conscious level. And often, the harder the orchestra and conductor try to make it right, the worse the music sounds.

At that point—the point when you know the tempo is off and the piece sounds a bit alien—everyone has to stop and examine how to rebuild trust. They also have to demonstrate trustworthiness.

Everyone has an equal role in the music. The conductor is not the boss, but rather an equal partner with a responsibility for coordination. Similarly, each member of the orchestra is an equal partner in making the music whole.

So how do you build, and rebuild, trust as well as show your own trustworthiness to make the music of your family whole? Building trust is an emotional, not an intellectual, process. Your mind isn't absent, but your thoughts support the process rather than dominate it.

Paul Zak is a neuroeconomist, so he has studied the brain and economics in an intertwined fashion. His pioneering work involves the mechanisms for building trust, which makes him sought after by executives who want to understand consumer behavior as well as improve workplace performance. Specifically, he's examined the role of a single biological substance in building trust, whether between strangers or people who know each other: oxytocin. In *The Moral Molecule: How Trust Works*, he covers the biochemistry of love, trust, empathy, and other conditions that allow us to feel connected to other people.

Zak has done experiments involving oxytocin and money that reveal heaps about how wonderful we can be as human beings—how much we can trust and invest in the welfare of perfect strangers. The point for our discussion is, if we can be this giving with someone we don't even know and never see, how much better can the expression be with someone we actually care about? What deep level of trust can we engender if we have the same biochemical mechanisms operating with a spouse, children, and stepchildren?

The challenge Zak faced in doing any experiments with oxytocin is that it doesn't flow abundantly in human beings in myriad circumstances. If human beings produced oxytocin at will and with ease, we might have world peace. Instead, there needs to be a significant stimulus for people to produce the hormone and when they do, it has a "three minute half life and it degrades rapidly at room temperature."[2] So, it's not as though he could fill a room with oxytocin mist to arouse feelings of well-being the way the Glenda the Good Witch woke up Dorothy in *The Wizard of Oz* by sending snow to the poppy field. Normally, oxytocin levels rise briefly during sex, birth, and breastfeeding. So Zak wondered how he could provoke a body to produce it in a controlled experiment and then evaluate what effect it had on a person's behavior.

He invited people to his lab, offering each one $10 to participate in a study. It involved drawing a few vials of blood and sitting around for about an hour and a half. All participants were matched into pairs by a computer; they didn't know or see each other during the experiment. One of them received a message asking, "Do you want to give up some of your $10 you earned for being here and ship it to someone else in the lab?" It was presented as a one-time opportunity with the result being that the gift would be tripled when the amount was deposited in the other person's account. So Person A had $10 and he was essentially told, "If you give all of this money to the stranger you've been paired up with, he'll get $30. If you give him $1, he'll get $3." The other person in the pair—we'll call him Person B—got a message if Person A chose to transfer money to him. The question posed to Person B was: "Do you want to keep all of what Person A sent you, or do you want to send some amount back?"

Experimental economists had run this test around the world, and for much higher stakes, and the consensus view was that the measure from the first person to the second was a measure of trust, and the transfer from the second person back to the first measured trustworthiness. But in fact, economists were flummoxed on why the second person would ever return any money. They assumed money is good, why not keep it all?

That's not what we found. We found 90 percent of the first decision-makers sent money, and of those who received money, 95 percent returned some of it. But why? Well, by measuring oxytocin we found that the more money the second person received, the more their brain produced oxytocin, and the more oxytocin on board, the more money they returned. So we have a biology of trustworthiness.[3]

Although the transactions in this experiment involved two people giving, taking, and giving back, the same fundamental principle applies in "pay it forward" behavior. That is, someone extends a kindness to you, whether it's financial or some other kind of generous behavior, and that act inspires you to give selflessly to someone else. In the movie *Pay It Forward*, a young boy takes his social studies teacher seriously in a challenge to "change the world" and, unwittingly, starts a movement in which each person who is helped unconditionally by a stranger helps three other people. This is a sort of "contact high," an almost contagious spread of good feelings associated with the release of oxytocin.

In Zak's situation, he realized his experiment had some methodological flaws. He had not actually proven that oxytocin caused or boosted trustworthiness just by measuring levels during the experiment. It looked that way, but he had to dig deeper and make sure it wasn't one of the other substances that oxytocin interacts with that was at work. Having eliminated that possibility through further research, he set out to design an experiment similar to the first wherein he administered oxytocin to some people and gave others a placebo. By doing so, he could determine a cause-and-effect relationship between the level of a person's trust/trustworthiness and the level of oxytocin in his system.

I found I could do it with a nasal inhaler. So along with colleagues in Zurich, we put 200 men on oxytocin or placebo, had that same trust test with money, and we found that those on oxytocin not only showed more trust, we can more than double the number of people who sent all their money to a stranger—all without altering mood or cognition.[4]

Zak's findings would have practical application if it were possible to give your family members a nasal inhaler with oxytocin mist before every family meeting. Barring that, you need to find old-fashioned mammalian ways to arouse production of this useful hormone. Because trust is something that you can *decide* to have, but it isn't something that exists in a real, functional way in your relationships unless you *feel* it.

Two big problems are that it takes good feelings to make the hormone—good begets better—and some people just don't have it in them. Regarding the latter, it's quite possible that you are trying to make positive connections in your relationships—you're kissing your spouse, hugging your children, and doing all of the things that are supposed to spark trust by arousing the production of oxytocin, and there is a member of your family who "doesn't feel the love." The sad-but-true reality is that some people do not respond with normal oxytocin production. Also, kids especially can often see right through inauthentic expressions of affection, so do a self-examination to be sure *you* believe you are trustworthy.

In her couples' and family practice, Trevor often explores the concept of "felt sense" with her clients. This concept, meaning the rich experience of your partner's feelings, was introduced in Chapter 3 in the story of Gabby and Mark. A component is the somatic experience of knowing where your feelings are located in your body. You might hold anxiety in your neck, for example, and you may not be aware of it unless someone points that out to you.

All emotions are registered in our bodies before they even get to the mind! If you understand and use the concept of felt sense, you have a powerful tool of both self-awareness and "us" awareness. In other words, you can use your body signals to give a first alert on how your relationships are doing.

Maryann does teaching and consulting related to body language. One of the first things she helps people see and understand is how emotions leak through changes in voice and body. A person skilled in reading body language may be able to tell the other person, "You're feeling stress," even before the individual realizes stress is present. A person who pays close attention to a loved one can often see it that early as well. Stress is a barrier to trust-building. Show you have the person's best interest at heart so she feels safe with you; together you will replace stress with a growing sense of trust.

Cindy brought a son to her marriage to Hannah, and then Cindy bore a little girl with her. Unfortunately, the child had a congenital heart issue and required a great deal of parental monitoring and medical care. Hannah found the range of parenting responsibilities overwhelming; she started drinking heavily. After a few months of this, Cindy gave her an ultimatum: rehab or divorce. Hannah chose a 30-day inpatient program.

When she came home, she didn't trust herself to stay sober. In fact, outside the bubble world of the residential treatment facility, she didn't trust herself to do much of anything. Cindy knew that Hannah would be incapable of being a loving partner and parent if she didn't trust and love herself. They went to couple's counseling. It took just a few sessions before Hannah felt she was adapting to life "outside the bubble." Once she started thinking about their life at home and with friends, she could rattle off all the ways Cindy had her back. It was the same with her eight-year-old stepson, whom they nicknamed "Red"; he stood shoulder-to-shoulder with his mom and looked out for Hannah.

Hannah and Cindy had a trust breakthrough. Neither one felt the need to overcompensate and spoil the music. A little thing—that was actually a big thing—that helped Hannah feel worthy of trust was when Red said he appreciated how she was always on time picking him up at school. Sometimes those gestures of consistency that we take for granted put other people at ease. We meet other people's expectations to "be there," and that makes them feel safe and able to share trust generously.

Philosopher Onora O'Neill has written several books addressing the critical role of trust in society and the route to rebuilding trust. She states:

> Trust, in the end, is distinctive, because it's given by other people. You can't rebuild what other people give you. You have to give them the basis for giving you their trust . . . so you have to provide usable evidence that you are trustworthy. How to do it?[5]

O'Neill focuses on vulnerability as the key. Here's an example. Anyone who has purchased something from Nordstrom knows that the store has a long-standing policy that you can return what is not suitable to you. Many of us seek out a commercial relationship with a store like Nordstrom because we are not made to feel guilty if we buy a dress online that we find later makes us look too old or too fat. Just put it back in the box and you get a credit—no questions asked. We trust that Nordstrom will behave in that manner, but here's the key to why we have confidence in the company and feel comfortable doing business with it: Nordstrom is vulnerable with us. If the store ever changes that policy, it would undermine a *relationship*. Simply by announcing a change in policy—and think about how many companies have done this!—the store makes us fear doing business with them. They are no longer trustworthy because they are no longer vulnerable. We make a judgment to withdraw.

Give your family visible, simple, and sufficient evidence that you are trustworthy and you will engender trust. Primarily, make yourself vulnerable.

POINTS TO CONSIDER

One couple we interviewed described how they introduced his two children and her two children to each other through play. The kids were very close in age, but had gone to different schools so they didn't know each other.

No one was forced to interact or even look at each other at these get-togethers. They went bowling. The next time, they had a barbeque and watched a movie. Neither parent emphasized bonding or even paying attention to each other. As a result, all four kids seemed relaxed; they were distracted by the activities and entertainment. This kind of interaction went on for a year. When their parents finally announced that they wanted to get married, the kids tensed up. All of this going-to-the-movies stuff worked really well, so why mess it up by making everyone move in together?

The kids had come to enjoy each other's company. They were relaxed around each other. When stress suddenly infiltrated their life, they vented their feelings with each other. That's another way of saying that they shared each other's feelings. Through simple acts of play, they had come to trust each other enough to be honest about how they felt.

Trust is the living embodiment of safety. It is feeling cherished for who you are—love without judgment. Trust is necessary for unconditional love.

NOTES

1. Charles Hazelwood, "Trusting the Ensemble," TEDGlobal 2011, Filmed July 2011; https://www.ted.com/talks/charles_hazlewood?language=en.

2. Paul J. Zak, "Trust, morality – and oxytocin," TEDGlobal 2011, Filmed July 2011; https://www.ted.com/talks/paul_zak_trust_morality_and_oxytocin.

3. Ibid.

4. Ibid.

5. Onora O'Neill, "What we don't understand about trust," TEDx Houses of Parliament, Filmed June 2013; https://www.ted.com/talks/onora_o_neill_what_we_don_t_understand_about_trust.

Chapter 7

Vulnerability and Emotional Strength

Brené Brown is well known for her research, writing, and speaking about the power of vulnerability. She has said that a quote from Theodore Roosevelt changed her life. Not wanting a statement like that to be overly dramatic, she explained: "Sometimes when you hear something when you need to hear it and you're ready to hear it, something shifts inside of you."[1]

She encountered the quote after she rose to prominence quickly, because her TED talk on vulnerability went viral. Suddenly she was doing interviews and articles and, as it happens so often, some people felt compelled to post harsh comments online—not about her work, but about *her*. Things like, "Of course she embraces imperfection. What choice does she have—look at how she looks." "I feel sorry for her kids." "Less research, more Botox." They could only be described as mean-spirited and irrelevant comments, but they hurt her feelings.

The Roosevelt quote, from a speech given at the Sorbonne on April 23, 1910, captured "everything I know about vulnerability,"[2] according to Brown. "It is not about winning. It is not about losing. It's about showing up and being seen." We thought the quote would be a helpful one for you, too, because you wouldn't be reading this book if you saw yourself as a perfect partner, perfect parent, and perfect stepparent. In other words, every once in a while, you're under attack—even if the criticism is coming from within.

Yet every day, you show up. You are seen. You are, to circle back to Brown's thesis, living a life that embodies vulnerability.

In trying to create a blended family, you are in the middle of the action. To use Roosevelt's words, you are "in the arena."

> It is not the critic who counts; not the man who points out how the strong man stumbles, or where the doer of deeds could have done them better. The credit

belongs to the man who is actually in the arena, whose face is marred by dust and sweat and blood; who strives valiantly; who errs, who comes short again and again, because there is no effort without error and shortcoming; but who does actually strive to do the deeds; who knows great enthusiasms, the great devotions; who spends himself in a worthy cause; who at the best knows in the end the triumph of high achievement, and who at the worst, if he fails, at least fails while daring greatly, so that his place shall never be with those cold and timid souls who neither know victory nor defeat.

Because you are in the arena, you are bound to come under fire. But who's taking shots at you? Brown asserts that the only people from whom you should accept feedback (or criticism) are also people who are in the arena. That does not include your husband's golf buddy or wife's best friend. An important factor in finding the power of vulnerability in your family relationships is building trust and compassion *among yourselves*—protecting each other—and shielding yourselves from what other people think. Those outsiders, smart and caring as they may be, are not in the arena.

A family counselor, your parents, and others in your life might have "special seats" in your arena, but the challenge of growing the power of vulnerability in your family is a challenge that only members of the family can meet.

WHAT IS VULNERABILITY?

How would you feel about looking at your distraught teenage stepdaughter in the eyes and not having any answers for her? Could you say: "I don't know how to help you right now. You know better than I do what you need. Please tell me." She might judge you. She might be annoyed with you. She might wonder if you're stupid or incompetent. But then again, it might be the most powerful parenting you could provide at the moment.

"I don't know" expresses vulnerability if you are in a position when you are "supposed to know." Unfortunately, when a person in authority such as a CEO, doctor, or parent says, "I don't know," people commonly interpret that as weakness.

Brown puts "weakness" at the top of the list of misconceptions of what vulnerability is.

Brené Brown's Myths of Vulnerability are as follows:

1. Vulnerability is weakness.
2. "I don't do vulnerability."
3. Vulnerability is letting it all hang out.[3]

In one of her presentations on the power of vulnerability, Brown noted that she was once asked by people interpreting her talk for the deaf if she had technical terms they needed to learn. She told them the word she would be using most was vulnerability. They then showed her the gesture in American Sign Language they would normally use for the word; it conveyed the concept "weak in the knees." Brown told that wasn't a fit, so they told there was only one other sign for vulnerability, and then they demonstrated it. Both hands appear to be opening a garment at the chest—in the context of her talk, it would surely convey the idea of exposing one's heart. It doesn't take courage to get weak in the knees, but it does take courage to expose your heart.

In contrast to the myths, Brown defines vulnerability as uncertainty, risk, and emotional exposure.[4] The name of her bestseller is a simple phrase from Roosevelt's quote that captures how she sees vulnerability: *Daring Greatly*.

Her years of research point sharply to the fact that Brown's perception of vulnerability was shared by people who made a transition from needing certainty, fearing risk, and wanting to shield themselves emotionally to being the people "in the arena": as a value, courageousness was more important than being successful.[5] That requires a great deal of clarity about your aims and intentions. You don't just *hope* to be a loving partner and parent, you *intend* to be that person. You hold "loving" as a core value and you aim to love your partner and children—no matter what.

HOW VULNERABILITY WORKS

Vulnerability is fueled by trust and powered by empathy. But it also enables trust and empathy to form.

It's easy to look at a previous marriage and give it a number: 1, 2, 3. As the numbers get bigger, the optimism about success in the marriage tends to get smaller. In embracing the power of vulnerability, it may help to give your *current* relationship different numbers as it moves through stages.

When you got together with your current partner, consider that your "first marriage." Perhaps this initial stage lasted a week, or maybe it lasted a year. Then something happened and there was a shake-up. Maybe not a big shake-up—or, then again, maybe it was something significant. After that, you have the opportunity for a second marriage. Same person; marriage number two. This is a process that can go on throughout your life together. And each time, the marriage begins anew when you and your partner show up for each other and are seen by each other, that is, when you are vulnerable with each other.

You can apply this model to your relationships with your children and step-children as well. Your interactions with them will change—and will probably feel like "new" relationships—as they go through the stages of growth toward adulthood. The way you show up for each other will evolve, and so will the way you see each other.

Let's revisit Brown's myths to see how people miss the opportunity to step up and be that courageous person in a relationship.

First, they refuse to send the messages "I don't know" or "I need your help." They are like the candidate for political office who cannot bring himself to admit he doesn't have all the solutions to his constituents' problems. His platform appears to have all the planks, but watch out: Some of those planks won't hold up if you walk across them. There is tremendous weakness in asserting you have all the answers and great strength in inviting someone you trust to help you find the answers.

Second, "I don't do vulnerability" is one of the most paranoid and self-destructive things anyone could believe. The fear and avoidance of intimate connection with another human being undermines effectiveness, happiness, and even health. In our book, *Forging Healthy Connections*, we focused on the well-documented necessity of interpersonal relationships to both physical and mental health. And the fact is, while people need autonomy to be fully functional as adult human beings, people need connections to sustain their health and well-being—and vulnerability is vital to connecting with another human being.

People we hold courageous "do" vulnerability. A list of courageous people in history would include Helen Keller, Nelson Mandela, and Mahatma Gandhi, all of whom had intimate connections with people with whom they allowed themselves to be vulnerable. Who are the courageous people in your life? Hopefully, you put yourself at the top of the list because you can't expect someone else to do vulnerability if you don't do it yourself.

Third, the assumption that vulnerability means letting it all hang out—telling the other person all of your deep, dark secrets—is false. You can tell all of your deep, dark secrets on your Facebook page and those admissions don't put you any closer to the power of vulnerability than does talking to yourself in a closet. "Vulnerability is about sharing our feelings and our experiences with people who have earned the right to hear them."[6]

Ben was 42 and a vice president at a pharmaceutical company when he met Marta, his VP counterpart at another pharmaceutical company. Both had PhDs, with Marta spending her early career doing medical research at a university. She felt compelled to make the jump to the corporate world because she was a single mom; the biological father of her child left her three months after their son was born. He also left his twelve-year-old daughter with her and took off for South America, never to be seen or heard by them again. Marta raised the daughter and then, facing bills for her college, accepted a lucrative position with a company mostly known for its work in vaccines. When the daughter was half way through college and her son, Tad, was in second grade, Marta and Ben married.

Ben's expertise was quality control. People in the company looked to him to have all the answers, and he seemed to have them. He found it difficult to be any different at home with Tad, who liked his stepfather—particularly because he made Marta so happy. But Tad didn't feel close to him. He didn't share stories about school or soccer practice. Basically, they were friendly toward each other and that's as far as the relationship went.

One day, Tad asked his mom and Ben for a puppy. Marta had no interest in having a dog around, but Ben suddenly got very animated. "What kind of puppy?" he asked Tad.

"I think maybe one that will grow up and be really big, like a Great Dane," Tad answered.

Without thinking through what Marta might have to say about this, Ben let out a big, "Yes!"

Marta rolled her eyes: "Can I have a word with you, Ben?" She turned to Tad and said that she and Ben just needed a minute alone.

"Where did that come from?" she asked Ben. He said that he had always wanted a dog, but his parents wouldn't allow it and he had led the life of a bachelor and corporate executive for so long that he never thought he could devote enough time to a dog. "So this is about you, not Tad," she said with a little smile. He admitted that was probably true, and vowed to help Tad take care of "the puppy." They agreed that Tad—and Ben—could have a dog.

Tad did a lot of homework on dog-parenting and by the time Giant joined the family, Ted felt he could handle anything—feeding, walking, playing, training. Ben, who seemed equally excited about having Giant in the family, knew absolutely nothing about caring for a puppy.

As it turned out, the eight-year-old who thought he knew everything about dogs and the guy in his mid-40s who thought he knew everything about everything found out that neither knew how to deal with a Great Dane puppy. They had to rely on each other every day for new insights and new information. Raising Giant helped them feel vulnerable with each other. It wasn't uncomfortable or emasculating. In fact, their reliance on each other and comfort with making mistakes with Giant helped them stand up straighter and stronger (emotionally speaking).

To say that their relationship went to a higher level is accurate. To say that their relationship was vital to creating a blended family is also accurate.

WHERE DOES VULNERABILITY LEAD?

Vistage is a company that enables chief executives to help each other improve their performance through peer-advisory groups and sharing experiences. They cannot be effective with each other unless they candidly disclose information about the way they function as CEOs. In other words, to create connections with significance, they must be vulnerable with each other.

For them, vulnerability is a threshold they must reach in order to get value out of their Vistage experience. It's analogous to a stage-gate in a product innovation process, meaning you can't get to the next phase of development until you pass through a "gate." Without going through the vulnerability gate, attempting the other steps in the self-improvement efforts is a waste of time; nothing else of quality happens.

For these executives, and for you in your relationships as a partner and parent, vulnerability leads to personal growth. It enables you to heal the wounds of past mistakes. If the head of a company feels lingering shame for being a party girl in college, firing someone she didn't like for no reason other than that she didn't like him, and cheating on her husband, then her self-worth is constantly taking hits. Somewhere in her mind, these terrible missteps make her unworthy of being a CEO. The logical outcome is that she will be a lousy CEO, unless and until she has people around that she trusts who say, "I've been there." They don't judge her, they understand her. They relate to her. They are as exposed as she is.

If a stepmother feels lingering shame for a messy divorce, for a few bad parenting choices with her own biological children, and for making her career a priority when her mother was dying, then she will be a lousy stepmother. She needs to go through the gate and bravely expose her heart to her partner and children to put that shame in its place—a trashcan of emotional junk. Shame wasn't useful when you first brought it into your life and it's never turned into anything useful in your life.

Brené Brown asserts that one of the greatest casualties of invulnerability is empathy—the subject of Chapter 8—and that empathy is the antidote to shame. As a segue to the next chapter, consider these words from her TED talk on shame:

> If you put shame in a Petri dish, it needs three things to grow exponentially: secrecy, silence and judgment. If you put the same amount of shame in a Petri dish and douse it with empathy, it can't survive. The two most powerful words when we're in struggle: Me, too.[7]

POINTS TO CONSIDER

Vulnerability requires courage and it reflects the presence of courage. The quality of your relationships depends on your squaring your shoulders and stepping into "the arena," that is, it requires the courage to show up and be seen. That is how you begin to harness the power of vulnerability with the members of your blended family.

NOTES

1. Brené Brown, "Why Your Critics Aren't The Ones Who Count," 99U presentation, Published December 4, 2013; https://www.youtube.com/watch?v=8-JXOnFOXQk.

2. Ibid.

3. Brené Brown, *Daring Greatly*, Gotham, 2012.

4. "Brené Brown on The Power of Being Vulnerable," interview by Jonathan Fields, Published on October 3, 2012; https://www.youtube.com/watch?v=Sd3DYvBGyFs.

5. Ibid.

6. Margarita Tartakovsky, quoting Brené Brown in "3 Myths about Vulnerability," PsychCentral; http://psychcentral.com/blog/archives/2012/08/29/3-myths-about-vulnerability/

7. Brené Brown, "Listening to Shame," TED2012, March 12, 2012; http://www.ted.com/talks/brene_brown_listening_to_shame?language=en#t-1214789.

Chapter 8

The Bridge to Empathy

The third of the five elements you need to succeed in your blended family is empathy.

In a 1997 article for the journal *Nurse Education Today*, the authors explored whether empathy is a naturally acquired ability that develops with maturity, or a skill that can be taught and learned.[1] Their conclusion provided no answer. They said that "empathy remains a poorly defined, multidimensional concept which still remains not fully identified."

We respectfully disagree with the authors of that paper. In all fairness, in the intervening years, neuroscience, psychology, and sociology (among other disciplines) have enlightened us about many emotions; among them is empathy. Therapists and other scientists have come a long way in learning how to describe it, discuss it, and help people wake up to the importance of it.

Ten years after that article was published, nursing scholar Theresa Wiseman also tackled the subject of empathy in nursing. Her conclusion was quite different from that of the other authors. In "Toward a Holistic Conceptualization of Empathy for Nursing Practice," Wiseman asserted that empathy has different forms and that these can be plotted along a continuum. She therefore sees empathy as dynamic:

> Empathy is not a single phenomenon. Four different forms of empathy were identified, namely, empathy as an incident, empathy as a way of knowing, empathy as a process, and empathy as a way of being.[2]

Wiseman's starting point was a common, if not classic, definition of empathy that had been in the nursing literature for decades: "the ability to perceive the meanings and feelings of another person, and to communicate that feeling to the other."[3] But her understanding took on new dimensions in the course of her study, which examined empathy in an oncology ward. Carried out over a two-year period, it involved both observations and interviews.

By looking at how Wiseman describes each of the forms of empathy, you'll get a sense of how the discussion in this chapter weaves them all into the discussion. The aim is to recognize the experience of all of them, knowing that empathy is dynamic, so the experience of it with your partner and your children and stepchildren will develop over time.

- Incidences of empathy: These are discrete episodes. In the context of Wiseman's study, they typically occurred during specific situations—for example, when a patient was being admitted, when bad news was being conveyed to a patient, or when treatment was being discussed.
  - ○ When your stepdaughter tells you she didn't get asked to the prom, your heart goes out to her. You weren't asked to the prom either and you have a flash of pain that matches hers. It's an incidence of empathy.
- Empathy as a way of knowing: Wiseman found that the incidences of empathy occurred more frequently between a nurse and a patient as they got to know each other better. She describes it as a less active and more passive experience than the initial one. It was something that became integral to their interaction.
  - ○ In the case of your stepdaughter, the two of you now have a sense that you can count on each other for understanding.
- Empathy as a process: With the integration of empathy into a nurse-patient relationship, the nurse got more practice feeling empathetic with that person. It became part of the process of providing support to that patient.
  - ○ With your stepdaughter, you aren't "waiting for a crisis" to share this emotion. Day-to-day living provides ongoing opportunities to connect through empathy.
- Empathy as a way of being: After she integrated empathy into several of her relationships with her patients, the nurse felt empathetic with a growing number of patients. Empathy then had a role in the person's nursing practice.
  - ○ Similarly, the emotional door you and your stepdaughter opened creates an opening—*for both of you*—for empathetic relationships with other members of the blended family.

LEARNING EMPATHY

In 1994, Maryann visited virtual reality labs in the San Francisco Bay area as part of her research for a book on the future of medicine. At one of the labs, a researcher equipped her with special gloves and goggles and told her she was going to perform gall bladder surgery. As primitive as the VR experience was—compared to now, anyway—she felt immersed in the activity of the operating theater. What she remembers is that opening her hand allowed her to get a scalpel or other instrument; opening it again with a tossing movement allowed her to discard it. Not being a surgeon, she killed her virtual patient, but the whole thing felt like a cartoon so it was pure fun, no trauma. In some ways, experiencing the movie *Avatar* felt more like a real situation; the ability to create immersion experiences had progressed steadily in the decades since her future-of-medicine research.

But the big difference between the lab experience of 1994 and seeing *Avatar* was her ability to control something in the environment. In the lab, she affected the story and determined the outcome.

This experience says something essential about the nature of empathy. It involves *action*. While sympathy is observing someone's pain and feeling for that person—"I'm so sorry your dog died!"—empathy is feeling *with* someone. It embodies an impulse to act on that feeling of connection; when you have empathy you have reached inside yourself and found the same pain the person you are empathizing with feels. You don't just watch the hurt, you feel it, too.

So throughout this discussion of empathy, we are talking about an emotional response that stimulates behavior that you believe will alleviate pain. Your actions *right this minute* have the potential to make someone else feel better when you connect in an empathetic way.

From Maryann's ancient-history experience of VR, fast forward to twenty-first-century technology, through which people like filmmaker and VR pioneer Chris Milk can immerse the prestigious audience at the Davos World Economic Forum into the plight of Syrian refugees. They don't just feel they are there, they feel the impulse to change the outcome—and they can. But not by opening or closing a gloved hand. They can change it by making a decision in the real world that will affect the lives of those refugees around them in virtual reality.

Milk calls VR "the ultimate empathy machine" and what he has accomplished can teach all of us, dealing with all kinds of challenges, what it means to see and feel things from another person's perspective. And that is essential for someone who is trying to contribute to the evolution of a blending family.

The big difference between observation of a situation and connecting with the sensations of the people in it is the difference between watching a movie and living the story.

The VR film that Malik showed to the attendees at Davos is called "Clouds Over Sidra," made in conjunction with the United Nations. His team went to a Syrian refugee camp in Jordan in December 2014 and shot the story of a twelve-year-old girl named Sidra. She and her family fled Syria through the desert to seek refuge in Jordan. Here is an excerpt from the film, with the young girl speaking:

> My name is Sidra. I am 12 years old. I am in the fifth grade. I am from Syria, in the Daraa Province, Inkhil City. I have lived here in the Zaatari camp in Jordan for the last year and a half. I have a big family: three brothers, one is a baby. He cries a lot. I asked my father if I cried when I was a baby and he says I did not. I think I was a stronger baby than my brother.[4]

Following this excerpt, in his TED Talk, Milk explained to the audience what the people at Davos experienced during the film.

> So, when you're inside of the headset . . . you're looking around through this world. You'll notice you see full 360 degrees, in all directions. And when you're sitting there in her room, watching her, you're not watching it through a television screen, you're not watching it through a window, you're sitting there with her. When you look down, you're sitting on the same ground that she's sitting on. And because of that, you feel her humanity in a deeper way. You empathize with her in a deeper way.

The intellectual process that many of us go through in trying to understand the point of view of another person in the household has its limits. An intellectual process involves data collection (watching, listening, touching), analysis of data, and some conclusion about what's happening. The immersive experience of VR means that you feel what is happening to the other person. Sure, you observe and analyze, but you are not just an observer or an analyzer. Your perception is that whatever is occurring is happening to *you*; you are in the context of another human being's experience.

How do you get to that place without Chris Milk's marvelous technology?

Hedy Schleifer and her husband of five decades, Yumi, are couples therapists. Schleifer does a moving and powerful presentation called "The Power of Connection" in which she talks about three invisible connectors: the space, the bridge, and the encounter. Her opening story encapsulates how all three help you transport to another person's world. The introductory portion of the story establishes her mother as a daring and bright woman who engineered an escape from a concentration camp in Vichy, France, that brought both her and her husband into Switzerland. After trekking through the Alps, quite literally she threw herself over the Swiss border, which was closed to immigrants, and then her husband smuggled himself into the country days later. A few months after that, in 1944, she gave birth to Hedy.

> Decades later, I'm sitting with my mother at an old age home in Israel and I cannot bear to see her. She is sitting in a wheel chair. She doesn't know who

I am. I feel guilty. I feel sad. I'm struggling. I'm angry. This is my hero! Why should she be here?

And I realize that I'm not visiting her. I'm with my own emotions. And I make a decision: I'm going to cross the bridge into the world of my mother. I will leave the world where I am struggling, and I will go and meet her. And I will bring with me new eyes.

And so I did. I came. I sat across from her. And I crossed the bridge and landed in her world. And I looked at her. And she looked at me. And in Yiddish, she said, "You are my daughter." And I started to cry. And with her hands, she gently wiped my tears.

She hadn't recognized me for months. Of course, I hadn't been there—emotionally.

This miracle with my mother illustrates the three invisible connectors.[5]

As Schleifer defines them, "space" is the relational space between two people. This concept emerges from the work of philosopher Martin Buber who described in his book *I and Thou* a space between human beings where relationships live. His implication is that a "relationship" doesn't reside in each of the people involved; it exists in the space they share together—the "sacred space." Each person has responsibility for the space. By introducing too much of your "stuff" into the space, as Schleifer says she did with her mother, the space is polluted. It's an uncomfortable feeling for both people. If that discomfort persists, these two people will not want to be around each other anymore.

The "bridge" is the connection between the worlds of those two people. Part of taking responsibility for the space is crossing that bridge. Leave everything behind when you start the journey: Figuratively speaking, you leave your shoes, your make-up, your resume, your rules, and, literally, you leave your prejudices, agenda, all the distraction of stories that show how clever or smart you are. Just leave them so you can intimately meet the person on the other side. The person might be your partner, your friend, your parent, your child, your stepchild. What do you do when you get there? Begin by listening.

Listening and paying attention are key tools of the encounter, which Schleifer calls the "connection of human essence to human essence."[6] In practical terms, this is how two people can achieve co-regulation. It is the phenomenon of "two limbic systems that resonate together,"[7] that is, a connection between two brains that helps each control basic emotions and have a positive effect on mood. This kind of interplay helps each person feel calm, safe, and loved. We need to repeat that it is *each* person, so this is not the occurrence of a parent offering words of comfort to a kid whose feelings are hurt. It is the parent and child sharing the experience; there may be no words involved at all.

In neuroscience terms, experiencing this level of intimate relationship is one way that two people can activate their mirror neurons. They feel empathy for each other.

THE SCIENCE OF EMPATHY

Research done in the early 1990s laid the foundation for the identification of mirror neurons a decade later. Giacomo Rizzolatti was doing work with macaque monkeys when he discovered that certain groups of neurons in the brain located behind the eyeballs fired both when a monkey performed an action *and* when the monkey watched someone else perform that same action. So these neurons perked up in response not only to a specific movement, but also to a goal or intention.[8] Rizzolatti and his team inspired a number of other neuroscientists to try and determine if mirror neurons were some kind of missing link in explaining our deeply emotional responses to the experiences of other human beings, even strangers. If people can relate on a physiological level to another person's experience as though they themselves were feeling it, then empathy can be explained as a phenomenon of our physical beings.

The researchers studied how the mirror neuron system functions in both monkeys and humans and then, in 2004, published "The Mirror-Neuron System." Their study suggests that mirror neurons help facilitate imitation as well as help mammals understand the meaning of actions.[9] Since that seminal work, mirror neurons have been considered by many neuroscientists to provide an explanation for empathy, with Vilayanur Ramachandran leading the movement to recognize them as what "makes us human."[10] They are credited with being the reason normal people feel pain when we see another person suffering, whether that suffering is physical, emotional, or psychological.

For example, when a friend of Maryann's was going through layoffs at a large computer company, she saw the manager of human resources at her facility having to deliver the news to the individuals affected by the corporate action. This HR professional was so shaken by other people's sudden trauma—with all of its financial, social, and emotional implications—that it overwhelmed her. After her first few meetings with those affected by the layoffs, she walked down the hall with her head hung low and she was sobbing. People around her were so moved, that even those whose badges she had just confiscated when she told them it was their last day made an effort to comfort her and care for her. They crossed the bridge into her space and made a connection.

Seeing a loved one in the hospital with needles strapped to his veins can send a chill through us. We experience a kind of pain, as though the needles were in our hand; to use Wiseman's terms, it's an incidence of empathy. We can even feel this very real, personal hurt when we watch a movie that has torture scenes in it. The sensation may be so intense that we have to take our eyes away from the screen.

However, just because the motor neurons in mammalian brains appear to enable the *capacity* for empathy, it does not mean that a person's emotions are automatically triggered. So, for example, a doctor might care deeply about a patient's suffering, but be able to maintain distance from it so she can do her job. The relationship between the presence and motor neurons and feeling someone's pain may not be as simple, then, as "You have them, therefore, you feel." Some scientists believe that their presence enables us to tune in to another person's feelings, but there isn't really a cause-and-effect relationship. It is the difference between being forced to be empathetic and making it possible to be empathetic. Therefore, we can think of empathy as a choice.

Since mirror neurons are behind the eyes, they seemed distinctly associated with the visual sense. What about blind people? Rizzolatti *et al.*, wondered this as well. Their study indicated that as long as people received enough information through other senses to have a clear idea of what was happening, their mirror-neuron system was also active.[11]

THE CHOICE OF EMPATHY

Part of how we connect and how deeply we share another person's experience is a natural expression of what we see, hear, and feel. Part of it is related to choices we make about what to focus on, as well as what "job" we have to do at the moment. You can't effectively manage a cardiac emergency, giving CPR and telling people around you what to do, if you are so emotional that your cognitive brain has shut down. Behaving efficiently in that situation doesn't mean you lack empathy; it means you recognize that thinking and acting are your priorities at the moment.

What Schleifer conveyed in her story was a conscious effort to activate mirror neurons so that she and her mother could have a shared experience. But notice that it was much more about joy than pain. That is the other beauty of empathy: We can feel deeply and truly happy together when something good happens.

Biological parenting automatically plants the seeds of empathy between parent and child because the giggling and burping of an infant trigger a sense of connection, warmth, and shared experience. But the cultivation of empathy requires that there be reinforcements throughout life. The trauma of a divorce, death, or abandonment can cause a child to be very fearful of interaction, to not believe that anyone understands her, much less is able to feel her joy and pain.

As a stepparent, be bold. In whatever words work for you, you can teach your wounded stepchild about "sacred space" between people, crossing the bridge, and encountering each other with open hearts. Don't be afraid to be explicit about how amazing it is to share another person's joy.

Maia Szalavitz is coauthor with child psychiatrist Bruce Perry of *Born for Love: Why Empathy is Essential—and Endangered.* For *Psychology Today*, she wrote an article called "The Joy of Empathy: Why It Matters & How to Teach It to Your Kids." She advises to make the implicit explicit:

> When we see kids smiling in response to others, point out how seeing someone else smile made them feel good; when we see that they enjoy our reaction to their artwork and gifts, praise them for being happy for us. Saying that "it's better to give than receive," may ring hollow—pointing out when children are actually experiencing the feeling of taking joy in giving is much more powerful.
>
> Allowing children to own this ability and recognize it in themselves will also encourage it—helping them to define themselves as the kind of people who are happy for other people will make them feel like good people, too. Encouraging such an identity will reinforce other positive behaviors as well. Changing behavior to suit an identity you prefer is actually one of the easiest ways to make changes.[12]

POINTS TO CONSIDER

A single mom posted the following story on Facebook:

> My daughter has not seen her biological dad since she was four. She's 11 now. When she was two he contacted me and asked if I would allow him to terminate his parental rights so he could stop paying child support and I agreed. I wanted to spare her the heartache of a revolving door father and the sacrifice of the financial support was well worth him never being able to disappoint her again. I never lied to her about where he went or who her dad was. I have always answered her questions in the most age appropriate way possible. When she was four he contacted me and told me he has been diagnosed with cancer and would like to see her. I set aside a day and we met in the park. He had asked for two hours. He stayed 20 minutes and we never heard from him again. Over the summer we ran into somebody that knows him and they commented on how she looks like his other children. They elaborated that he has settled down and has a family now. My stomach tied itself in knots thinking of how hurtful that must be to my daughter. I cut the conversation short and we got in the car to leave and that's when I saw her smiling. She said "Mom . . . he figured out how to be a dad. That's such a nice thing. I'm happy for his kids." And that's the day an 11-year-old taught me all I need to know about forgiveness.[13]

The story illustrates the behavior of a securely attached child who has been loved and who therefore has the capacity to feel empathy for a dad who has hurt her. It would suggest that, for her, empathy is "a way of being," as Wiseman described. Her mother gave her a beautiful emotional foundation for living a life with a mature sense of compassion. All of us need to keep moving in that direction with each other and with our children and stepchildren.

NOTES

1. Vincent Price and John Archbold, "What's it all about, empathy?" *Nurse Education Today* 17(2) (April 1009): 106–110.

2. Theresa Wiseman, "Toward a Holistic Conceptualization of Empathy for Nursing Practice," *Advances in Nursing Science* 30(3) (2007): E61–E72. http://www.researchgate.net/profile/Theresa_Wiseman/publication/6136896_Toward_a_holistic_conceptualization_of_empathy_for_nursing_practice/links/09e4150f6a4127a969000000.pdf.

3. J. Gagan, "Methodological notes on empathy," *Advances in Nursing Science* 5(2) (1983): 65–73.

4. Chris Milk, "How Virtual Reality Can Create the Ultimate Empathy Machine," TEDGlobal 2015, Filmed March 2015; https://www.ted.com/talks/chris_milk_how_virtual_reality_can_create_the_ultimate_empathy_machine?language=en.

5. Hedy Schleifer, "The Power of Connection," TEDxTelAviv, April 26, 2010.

6. Ibid.

7. Ibid.

8 GiacomoRizzolatti and LailaCraighero, "The Mirror-Neuron System," *Annual Review of Neuroscience* 27 (2004):169–192; http://www.kuleuven.be/mirrorneuronsystem/readinglist/Rizzolatti%20&%20Craighero%202004%20-%20The%20MNS%20-%20ARN.pdf.

9. Ibid.

10. Christian Jarrett, PhD, "Mirror Neurons: The Most Hyped Concept in Neuroscience?" *Psychology Today*, December 10, 2012; http://www.psychologytoday.com/blog/brain-myths/201212/mirror-neurons-the-most-hyped-concept-in-neuroscience.

11. Ibid.

12. Maia Szalavitz, "The Joy of Empathy: Why It matters & How to Teach It to Your Kids," *Psychology Today*, posted March 29, 2010 in Born for Love; https://www.psychologytoday.com/blog/born-love/201003/the-joy-empathy-why-it-matters-how-teach-it-your-kids.

13. https://www.facebook.com/cannonliz/posts/10205839596241444.

Chapter 9

Truth as a Gateway

Most people lie only if they have a reason to do it. Unfortunately, there are lots of reasons, like feeling judged, inadequate, or misunderstood. In a home where people share trust, vulnerability, and empathy, those reasons disappear. Truthfulness becomes a default behavior. Truth is a gateway back to trust, vulnerability, and empathy; they all work together.

We realize that, in some situations, being truthful is a frightening prospect. In anxiously attached relationships, it is often hard for a partner or a child to tell the truth. The withdrawer may be bullied into saying only what's "acceptable" and being completely honest feels like—or may actually be—a matter of life or death. That person may learn to stay silent, compliant, and agreeable as a matter of survival. That person is often a woman, who sees telling the truth as a dangerous activity, and lies as necessary tools to ensure *status quo* at home.

Safe relationships are about being able to tell your truth. A relationship is safe when the truth is met with empathy and love.

DEFINING TRUTH

When accident investigators want to find out what happened, they often interview people at the scene. The stories might be different depending on the witness's location, for example. When the investigators piece together the information, do they have the truth? No. They have a collection of facts, or what they hope are facts. The truth is the honest story each person told and that tends to include interpretations, reactions, and speculation.

A number of years ago in Minneapolis, a woman went through a red light and collided with a car proceeding through the intersection. When police asked the person whose car was hit what happened, she said she was struck at slow speed by a car that had gone through the red light. She was frightened, but okay, so she got out of her car and ran to the other vehicle because she saw the driver was slumped over the wheel. She said she knew immediately that something bad must have happened to the driver to cause the accident because she was her high school math teacher.

The facts were that a car went through a red light at slow speed and struck a car in the intersection. The truth for the victim was that she was frightened when it happened and soon knew "something bad must have happened" to the other driver because, in her mind, she believed that her high school math teacher would never have just ignored a red light. The driver's truth also contained an invisible fact: Her teacher had suffered a fatal heart attack at the wheel, so "something bad" had indeed happened.

Biases like that of the woman in the car crash can also result in a distortion of the facts. When the bias is buried in the subconscious, the person is still telling the truth. A person who believes she's telling the truth would pass a lie detector test regardless of how wrong she might be about the facts. But when the bias is in the person's conscious mind, it can be the reason a person knowingly distorts the facts. (The officer asks, "Did you see your friend draw his gun on the shop owner?" The gang member replies, "The guy had a gun! It was self-defense!" The reality is that the shop owner did have a gun but he hadn't drawn it yet.)

Let's say it wasn't the victim in the crash who knew the other driver, but rather a witness on the sidewalk. She saw nothing but the impact, and ran over to see if she could help. She recognized the math teacher, who is someone she respected. When the police asked her what she saw, she recounted the facts, but added that "something bad must have happened" to the driver to cause her to go through the red light. That's pure speculation, but she felt compelled to weave it into her account in an attempt to preserve the reputation of the teacher. Her sense of loyalty shaped her truth.

In *Nothing But the Truth*, here is how Maryann defines truth—a distinctly human experience:

> Truth is rooted in fact, but personal imagination, beliefs, and experiences affect how we process the facts. Emotions and interpretations are therefore parts of the spectrum that compose the truth. If we're missing some of the facts and/ or missing the human responses to them, then the truth has eluded us. Just as the opposite of "fact" may be "lie," the opposite of "truth" could be defined as "inability to see the whole."
>
> Because of our imagination, beliefs and experiences, human beings are capable of synthesizing ideas and points of view in a way that transcends mere computer-like analysis of data points. We don't just sort the data, organizing

them into neat columns; we make sense of them. We connect facts and ideas in uniquely personal ways to arrive at the truth.[1]

TELLING YOUR TRUTH

What you perceive as truth brings at least three factors into play: imagination, belief, and experience. Sometimes, imagination means that you "connect the dots" in a situation and your picture is a bird when it really should be a star. Belief is also very tricky because parents, teachers, preachers, and others in a position to influence your head and heart at a young age can imbue you with ideas and attitudes that you embrace as part of your truth. And even for the most logical and objective individual, personal experience will affect your truth.

Since truth encompasses personal realities as well as objective facts, people who've experienced the same thing can have different stories. Emotion plays a major factor in this. An ordinary way this might surface is the events-of-the-day conversation a couple might have in the evening. Sue comes home from an uneventful day at the office. It was nothing but a staff meeting, a hundred emails, editing a report for her boss, and a few cups of coffee. Her husband Al asks, "How was your day?"

"Boring," she says, "How was yours?"

"Awful!" He tells her that a colleague let loose at a meeting, criticizing him for cost-overruns on a project. Sue can tell: This guy's lashing out hurt my husband's feelings. It ruined his day.

If you were to ask anyone else who was with Al at the meeting, what his colleague said was inane and a blip in the discussion. But in fact, if the critical remark were excised from Al's experience, he would have told his wife it was a pretty good day. He would have mentioned the compliment a board member gave him on his last presentation and how delighted he was that a friend from college called. But his colleague was a buzzkill, so Al's truth became that he had an awful day.

Emotion can also contribute to a memory phenomenon called "misattribution," that is, you link an event to something to which it has no connection. You hear a woman raising her voice in a grocery store: "I told you not to touch the grapes!" You turn around and see a little boy holding his arm as though someone smacked him. You are horrified because, by all appearances, the woman just struck her child in the grocery store. If asked about the incident, that's your memory and every time you think of it, you feel horrified all over again. The real story is that the child ran into the side of a display rack after he snagged a couple of grapes and was trying to run away from the scene of the crime.

DEALING WITH LIES

When a child lies to an adult, the impulse for many adults is to discipline the child. It's a Ten Commandments approach: Lying is immoral, therefore, the aftermath of lying should be punishment. While you don't want to do anything to condone lying, ask yourself why a child, or an adult, would lie to you.

First, if the child is very young, he might just be confused about what to say when you ask, "Did you put that mark on the wall?" If your tone of voice is harsh, he might think the right answer is "No!"

Second, if the child is a post-toddler but is less than 7, she's at that age when imaginary friends move into the house and every night she turns into Disney princess. Along with that gift of being able to shift between fantasy and reality might come some statements that sound like lies to an adult. And yet, sometime during this period, the child should start to understand what it means to lie.

By the time the child is in the age bracket we're focusing on in this book, you can be rather certain that he or she can identify a lie. At that point, one of these reasons might apply:

- Cover up a mistake—Your stepson dented the fender of your car by backing into a light pole, but lied and said that someone must have hit the car while he was parked at the mall.
- Avoid feeling shame—Your stepdaughter lies about having sex because her biological father trained her to think that premarital sex will make her a slut.
- Impress you—You're the new person in the house and your stepson wants you to know you should be darned proud of being under the same roof as he is; you need to know what a football star he is.
- Manipulate your emotions—Once you hear what your stepdaughter has to say about her biological father, you will hate him, too.
- Gain a short-term advantage—Your child and stepchild agree that they will tell you they did their homework so they can both get out of doing their homework.
- See how gullible you are—It's a version of a practical joke that isn't funny. Your daughter tells you she got a tattoo because she knows that will make you crazy. She thinks it's funny when you foam at the mouth.

A child might also be emulating you when she lies. You call in sick when you're not to get out of going to work, so why can't she have a "sick day" to stay home and watch movies?

There are other reasons, but some of them indicate aberrant cognitive and emotional processing. That's a relatively rare situation, and not something that should be addressed in this context. If you notice that your child or stepchild seems to lie a great deal when there is no "good" reason like covering up a mistake or attempting to get out of homework, then it's time to see a counselor.

Since we have been talking a lot about the necessity and benefits of trust, vulnerability, and empathy, you probably have guessed right if you think we are *not* going to advise you to spank a lying child or put him in a closet! We recommend a few things that should elicit and encourage truthfulness through trust, vulnerability, and empathy.

1. Show your honest self. Body language and security expert Paul Ekman (*Telling Lies*) addressed his personal commitment to truthfulness on NPR's Radiolab in a segment called "Catching Liars." He told the host:

    When my daughter was born 27 years ago, I decided that I would take on as a life task to see if I could lead my life without lying. . . . I'm always looking for a way to see if I can solve a problem. It makes it more interesting. Just telling a lie is really dull. . . . Most of the time we lie out of laziness or timidity.[2]

    It's probably unrealistic to expect yourself to be a lifelong, creative truth teller like Ekman, but if you want to make truthfulness a default response in your home, then you have to set a good example.

2. Don't jump to conclusions. If you think your child has lied to you, find out if you're correct. Remember that emotions can profoundly affect a person's memory of an event. If the child was in an excited state when the event in question happened—and that could be happy, sad, scared, angry, disgusted, or surprised—then it's possible his memory of it is a little off. It's also possible he's tampering with the facts to create a better story, but you may not necessarily know.

    This is a great time to focus on the child's feeling and to be empathetic. If he has doctored the facts, and he feels you truly relate to what he felt and experienced when the event occurred, then you've just removed lots of reasons to lie.

3. Dig for the *real* reason behind the lie. Your stepchild may have grown up in a household where the first response to an accident like breaking a glass was, "Why did you do that?!" followed by a long time-out. So the lie to you about making a mistake might seem like a simple case of cover-up, but the emotion behind the cover up is fear. Or you might find it odd and unnecessary for a child that's popular and an accomplished athlete, for example, to embellish his accomplishments. Maybe he spent years feeling that no one listened to him, or that he was loved conditionally only when he achieved. His lies to sound a little better, a little more accomplished, might have come out of the avoidant style of one or both biological parents.

You probably won't get the answer to the real reasons for a while. When he knows he can trust you and feel vulnerable with you, you'll start to see progress.

4. Never call the child a liar. Never. Brené Brown makes a big distinction between guilt and shame, with guilt relating to an act and shame reflecting a sense of being. It's fine if a child feels guilty about lying; it's not at all acceptable if the child feels he is a liar. The latter is a feeling of shame and it's life-damaging, at least until the person can eliminate the feeling.

When a partner lies to you, the same advice applies. Your personal honesty, compassion, giving the benefit of the doubt whenever possible, and avoiding name-calling give your partner reasons to be truthful.

POINTS TO CONSIDER

We launched this chapter with a note about truth being a gateway back to trust, vulnerability, and empathy. As a corollary, truthfulness with your partner, children, and stepchildren results in the kind of emotional and mental health that you need to create a blended family. Truthfulness as a default behavior for everyone in your blend means you've all done the work!

NOTES

1. Maryann Karinch, *Nothing But the Truth*, Career Press, 2015, p. 20.
2. Paul Ekman, as recorded for "Catching Liars," Radiolab, National Public Radio; http://www.radiolab.org/story/91613-catching-liars/

Chapter 10

Structure with Feeling

Kids invariably ask "why." One of the persistent "whys" in many homes is about structure—rules, rituals, boundaries, and systems that place requirements on the child to behave or communicate a certain way. The "why" comes when the requirement doesn't seem to make sense.

Many times, children have a gut reaction to structure that gives adults major clues about its shortcomings, or about the gaps in a child's understanding of why a requirement actually does make sense. Kids tend to question or rebel against rules or practices that seem arbitrary because they have no apparent link to beliefs, values, and priorities in the home. The child asks, "Why?" and the unsatisfying answer is, "Because I said so!"

We don't mean to suggest that you should unearth the deep psychological meaning of every household rule; sometimes, you make a rule out of a basic need to keep your family organized. We do think it's important to give age-appropriate explanations when asked, however. When a twelve-year-old asks, "Why do we have to visit great-grandma every other Sunday?" you can give her a more substantive answer than you give your three-year-old. You can say, "Your great-grandma is suffering from Alzheimer's disease, which causes her to lose her memory and it gets worse all the time. She still knows who you are, but one day soon, she won't recognize you. Seeing you makes her very happy. Seeing her family together makes her very happy, and she feels loved." The last two sentences are probably all that you would use with a three-year-old.

Structure supports your ability to cocreate the "two Bs" with your partner—belonging and belief—just as trust, vulnerability, empathy, and truthfulness support it. The kind of structure you put in place in your home can help every person in your family feel as though he or she belongs and is loved. Your rules, requirements, boundaries, and systems help solidify the belief that you are in the adventure of blending together.

STRUCTURE AS A NECESSITY

Blending usually involves uncertainty for everyone involved. Both kids and parents had expectations and ways of going about daily life that will change in some way. Putting structure in place removes some of the wobbliness that people in the new family might feel with each other.

We interviewed one mom from a household where the dad, who was the biological father to two of the three children in their home, hated rules. His strict and very religious parents were fortunate to have five healthy sons who excelled in school, but four out of the five decided that their kids would never have to live with such rigidity. (The fifth replicated his upbringing.) As a result, she was never able to implement the kind of household practices that she wanted. In her family of origin, dinner was at 6:30 and everyone showed up unless there was a play rehearsal or gymnastics practice. In her family, everyone went on vacations together until the kids were 16. And in her family, rude or irresponsible behavior meant a sit-down with mother and dad to learn why that should never happen again.

Figuratively speaking, her child and stepchildren danced to their own, cacophonous, music. The lack of routine, rules, expectations of behavior, and boundaries regarding visits with the biological mom became their family norm. By the time they were 16, 14, and 12, they led their own lives for the most part. Except on holidays, they ate when they wanted and what they wanted; the upside of that was that one of them found his talent and became a chef. Except for special occasions, they could opt out of family-related events and hang out with their friends at someone else's house. Or, as happened with one of them, just shut himself in his room and avoid the scene downstairs.

The blend was not supported by the kinds of practices that generally remind family members that they are members of a family. To return to the musical metaphor, everyone in the chorus performed to his to her own song.

The contrasting situation is no better in achieving a blended family.

Steve had a successful pediatric practice, two children a year apart, a beautiful wife, and a string of affairs. He found it easy to recruit new lovers from the supply of moms who found his devoted concern for their children endearing. As far as some of them were concerned, he showed more genuine interest in them and their kids than their husbands.

Knowing that Steve had been adulterous their entire marriage, the wife asked for a divorce so she could be with the man she'd fallen for. She had waited until their daughter was 12 and their son was 13 before venturing outside the marriage; once she did, she announced her plan to move to the West Coast and remarry. She wanted the children to remain with their father in their current schools in Maryland and visit her periodically. Steve agreed that it would be best for the kids to stay where they were.

Steve's life was shaken up by the presence of two demanding teenagers. Within months, he began dating Clare, a woman in her late 30s, who desperately wanted to be a mother. She was unable to have children, so it was a dream come true when Steve asked her to marry him and become a parent to Lauren and Josh.

Clare tried to do everything right: Shuttle the kids to school activities, prepare healthy lunches, host gatherings at the house, help with homework. This freed Steve to focus on his practice and resume his extramarital adventures.

The kids didn't really think of Clare as a parent. In fact, when Josh introduced her to his new baseball coach when he entered tenth grade, he said, "This is Clare, my dad's wife." She was deeply hurt, but figured that everyone just needed time to grow together as a family.

Throughout high school, all the household systems ran smoothly. Steve and Clare seemed to collaborate well when it came to parenting issues; the kids got excellent grades. They both had their eyes on medical school, with Lauren stating openly that she wanted to go into practice with her father someday.

It was a family with all of the structure in place: boundaries, rules, routines, expectations, and systems of communication. What they lacked were the emotional underpinnings that give that structure purpose and quality. Trust, vulnerability, empathy, and truthfulness are not one-way streets, as Clare painfully learned in her years of trying to build a home with stepchildren and a husband who happily received, but rarely gave back.

Clare was hired help. A nanny with a wedding ring from the boss. By the time Lauren and Josh were starting to look at medical school, she opened her eyes to her situation and realized that there was no blended family: There was the family of Steve and his kids, and she just happened to share their house.

In this case, structure served an important function in the lives of the children, but it did not come out of Clare's and Steve's mutual desire to create a smooth-running home together. In terms of blending, a big red flag goes up when the children and their needs are the prime factor in how the household runs.

As we've said throughout the book, the couple must be at the center of blend. The couple is the most important system in a blended family.

STRUCTURE AS A FACTOR IN BLENDING

Blended families instantly have more stresses on them than traditional families. So whereas a family of two biological parents who have a couple of kids together moves through stages together and may develop rituals and rules over time, blended families often have to implement such elements of structure immediately. The presence of ex-partners complicates the challenge because the couple at the center of the blend also needs to agree on boundaries related to them. The boundaries range from visitation times, to the nature of co-parenting and how the stepparent supports the arrangement, to how kids talk about an absent parent.

In an article covering the unique challenges of blended families, couples therapist Mark Anderson noted:

> Traditional couples, for example, will acquire debt over time. They will also acquire children over time, waiting an average of two to four years before adding each additional child. They will also add life stressors, such as owning a home and making car payments, over time.
>
> While each of these events is stressful, spreading them out over time gives the couple the ability to adjust and adapt slowly. But for the stepcouple, all of these stressors, much like a damn breaking, occur all at once.[1]

Anderson was moved to write his article for the same reason that we were moved to write this book: According to the United States Bureau of Census, 1,300 stepfamilies are formed every day, meaning that roughly half of all households in the United States include stepparents and stepchildren. Both Anderson and Trevor have seen in their practices a rise in couples seeking counseling to cope with the stresses they suddenly find themselves facing, in their attempt to blend households. The focus has always got to be on what it takes to nurture love and everyone's faith that the home is a safe haven. Invariably, the conversation about "what it takes" encompasses the household systems that make life a little more predictable. When people in the household have confidence that certain expectations about privacy, meals, school activities, visits from relatives, and so on will be met, stress is mitigated. Comfort levels among the people in the blended family can rise normally. It may still take five to seven years for the blend to form fully, but it will be a steady process during which time there should be growth in everyone's ability to trust, be vulnerable, share empathy, and default to truthfulness. And during those years, as a result of everyone's personal growth, some of the rules, rituals, and expectations are bound to morph.

One of the people that we enjoyed interviewing had a great deal to say about the role of structure in how she and her husband created a blended family of eight kids. For the record, that's two more than the blended family in *The Brady Bunch*.

Brian's daughter was 9, just four months older than Debbie's daughter, when they met. His son was 5. Debbie and Brian dated for three years before they decided to undertake their blend, and they went into it knowing that they would also like to have children together.

Their big challenge the first year was the girls. Brian's daughter, Holly, considered herself a princess, so it was a little hard for her to suddenly be on equal footing with Debbie's daughter, Lynn. One of the first boundaries that Brian had to embrace was that Holly would get the same allowance and privileges as her stepsister, who was in the same class in school. The complicating factor was trying to co-parent with Holly's biological mother, who also treated her daughter as a princess. Invariably, Holly would come back from a weekend with her mother with new clothes or a new tennis racket or a new something else—a something else that Lynn didn't have. Lynn's biological father was a completely absentee parent, so she got resentful that she didn't have anyone treating her like a princess! The two girls made deliberate attempts to cause trouble between their parents with Holly determined to continue having princess treatment and Lynn alternately wanting the same thing and not wanting Holly to have it.

Needless to say, Debbie and Brian had a hard time enforcing the equal-treatment element of the relationship with their daughters. But Debbie stepped up to the challenge: "I was unapologetic. I told Brian this wouldn't work if we had a princess running the household. What we needed was a king and queen—and we were it." Brian asked his ex to cooperate and she reluctantly agreed to stop the shopping sprees.

Ultimately, it wasn't the household policy that caused a shift in the relationship between the two girls, though. It did help in that it reminded them that their parents saw them as equals, but spending time together made them want to *be* equals. Within a year, they started to dress very similarly and exchanged clothes on a regular basis. They were better than equals: They were sisters.

The girls were 13 and Brian's son, Seth, was 10 when Debbie and Brian had their first child together; four more followed in rapid succession.

In the next few years, the children found themselves with additional rules, routines, expectations, and boundaries coming into play. The huge emotional upside was that the structure contributed to a sense of amalgamation and belonging. Even when Brian's son and daughter gave her push-back— "You're not my mother!"—she kept things on track by saying, "I'm the adult in this situation." This is precisely the kind of clarity that helps a blending family keep moving forward, with family structure supporting the progress.

She also avoided the "do this, don't do that" dictum by saying to her kids/ stepkids and their friends, "In this house, we don't . . ." So that when friends of the children visited, which was often, they temporarily became part of the family—at least in terms of the rules. They knew rules like "In this house, we don't chew gum in the living room" and "In this house, we don't swear."

One of the house rules that Debbie says helped her avoid nagging was this: Until beds were made in the morning and everyone was dressed, no one had food. A violation—meaning someone lied about the bed being made—meant a $10 penalty. Right off the top of his or her allowance, that child handed over a $10 bill. That happened twice before there was total compliance.

Debbie and Brian thoughtfully and deliberately gave their eight children a sense of stability and security. And then Debbie added another dimension to the experience, which required a few more rules that the kids involved really enjoyed: She homeschooled her youngest few children. After seeing the older kids come home without the light of curiosity in their eyes, she decided there must be some better way for her children to learn. She had the education and commitment to homeschool and has been doing it for several years as of this writing. The fact is, Debbie could never have undertaken such a monumental challenge if she and Brian had not laid the foundation for a smooth-running household. The structure of their blended family supported some amazing learning opportunities for the youngest children.

Finally, even with that many children under a single roof, there is at least one moment in the day when the kids have alone time with a parent. Every night, each child chooses a favorite prayer—the littlest preferred "Twinkle, twinkle, little star" for a few months—and says it with mom/stepmom and/or dad/stepdad. The time together has the dual function of giving parent and child a private moment together and bringing the day to a relaxing end. The conflicts of the day are officially over.

As the kids got older, of course, that routine was harder to maintain, but it was never something that Debbie and Brian enforced. This was a moment that the kids enjoyed and it's something that the older two, who now have children of their own, have continued in their homes.

The structure that Debbie and Brian have in their home helps everyone feel the rhythm of the day. Unlike the family with no rules that we described above, the parents and children in this home have been dancing to the same music for years.

POINTS TO CONSIDER

In a beautiful blend, everyone comes to forget that some people have biological ties and some don't. What matters is the love they share and the synchronicity in their interactions. For a family, any family, having a sense of "how we do things in this house" helps engender a deep sense of connection.

NOTE

1. Mark Anderson, "Keepin' Love Alive: Stepfamilies," Scottsbluff Star Herald, August 24, 2015; http://www.starherald.com/entertainment/columns/keepin-love-alive-stepfamilies/article_4ef70f82-5b0b-5a5d-af69-350378d05bbd.html?mode=jqm.

Part III

STORIES AND
PRACTICAL INSIGHTS

Since you have gotten this far in our book, we can assume that you must be seriously considering blending or that you and your partner are already in the process. If you are blending now or "in the weeds" at this moment, trying to meet the daily demands of bringing a sense of belonging to the people under your roof, take time to give yourself love, empathy, and appreciation.

Stepparenting is one of the least appreciated activities ever. In fact it has been historically maligned; we have all grown up with the 'wicked stepmother' in *Cinderella.* Your story doesn't have to be anything like that.

Remember that you only need to get it right about 30 percent of the time. That is a forgiving number. If you can be kind to yourself, and have self-compassion, you will be a better parent, stepparent, and partner. Cultivate a soft approach to the way you speak to yourself, recognize what you are doing is extraordinary and important.

Shaping young people, growing love, and giving the future a new generation of caring, generous people is an important endeavor. In fact it is *the* most important job any of us can have. Doing it, as you have chosen to do, for nonbiologically connected people, is challenging and even more satisfying when things go well. Be sure to relish the joy of it and notice that you have done something special and beautiful.

Chapter 11

Challenges, Options, and Solutions

The following case studies developed out of in-depth interviews with four blended families, with two stories merged into one because there were many parallels. Two of the stories involved blends over three generations. This is a circumstance that our interviews and research indicate is quite common.

Names and some of the identifying circumstances have been changed to protect the identities of the family. There is an interesting point, however, to be noted about the names involved in the case studies. Over and over again, we saw that the person in the story who caused the family the most pain was not initially referred to by name. Sometimes, we found out the person's name only when we asked what the person's name was. The person had a title like "my ex" or "my mother's new husband," but he or she was like the evil Lord Voldemort in the *Harry Potter* books: "He-Who-Must-Not-Be-Named." This is an easy pattern to understand: If there is someone in your life you feel has dehumanized you, a natural response is to dehumanize that individual by not using his or her name. Calling an individual by name opens a window to empathy; there is at least a trace amount of personhood that you recognize in the offending party.

In family stories of trauma and challenge, it is quite common that a central player is self-absorbed. It is his or her anxieties, vengeance, agenda, or drama that sucks the health out of the home environment and gets that individual's primary attention. Children are secondary, as are any other people in the home. Once others in the home get some physical distance between themselves and that person, they also have the desire for the emotional distance that can come by not referring to the person by name.

With the case studies in this chapter, we have provided introductory and concluding insights to point out how attachment styles of the parents and stepparents played into the outcome. We have also woven commentary into the text on the challenges, options, and solutions.

Since these are real people, there are some loose ends and, with some events, a lack of resolution. That's because the stories are continuing to develop and there may be no resolution to certain issues for quite some time. We do some speculation in those cases, that is, based on what's happened so far, we project what might happen next.

At the end of the chapter, we have also included three stories of challenges to a family that resulted in options and solutions that were a little unconventional. All three blends worked, though, so that it's clear that a strong family unit can begin and evolve in various ways. In many, many cases, it isn't man *plus* woman *plus* kids *plus or minus* ex-partners *equals* blended family. The variations are nearly endless.

STORY A

Karen—stepmother of three girls and mother of two younger boys; secure parenting style with her own children, but somewhat anxious with her stepchildren

Jon—biological father of five; avoidant parenting style

Chris—biological mother of the three girls; chaotic parenting style

Central challenge—Oldest daughter of Jon and Chris has serious behavioral issues; same tendencies surfacing in other two girls

When Karen and Jon married, Jon's three daughters were ages 2, 5, and 6. They lived near Chris, the girls' biological mother, and so the two oldest visited them every other weekend. Chris insisted it would be better to wait a couple of years before the youngest came for visits and Jon agreed. This was a mistake. Jon went along with the proposal because he wanted to avoid any confrontation with Chris, but by doing that, he was also avoiding contact with his youngest daughter. Three years later, Karen and Jon moved a thousand miles from Temecula, California, to Colorado Springs, Colorado.

A year later the oldest daughter, Bethany, started having behavioral issues. That was the first time she came to live with Karen and Jon. She went from an environment with no rules to a home with rules, where she was expected to help out with household chores, do her homework on time, and be considerate to other people. Her father and stepmother also enforced table manners, which was something she did not acquire at her mother's house. Chris's career in residential real estate generally meant she was out of the house in the early evenings and Saturdays and the babysitter didn't cook.

She did fairly well that first year in Colorado, living with Karen and Jon throughout the school year. Jon, an orthopedic surgeon, had long hours, but a fairly regular schedule that got him home by around six o'clock every weekday evening. Karen worked at home as a freelance writer and editor. The three of them had dinner together almost every night; Karen's and Jon's son was one-year-old at the time.

At the end of the school year, Bethany went back to her mother's house and the behavior problems resurfaced. But Bethany's mom kept Bethany at her house thinking that she could "fix the problem" without having her daughter bounce back and forth between homes.

Sessions with a psychiatrist seemed to do nothing but build Bethany's resentment about the way she was treated: "No one understands me." Her rejection of the doctor's help and her mother's attempts to rein her in were part of a pattern that was becoming more and more ingrained: It's everyone else's fault. Bethany took zero personal responsibility for her actions.

Since Chris tended to emphasize the downside of things, Karen and Jon assumed she was exaggerating about her daughter's bad behavior. They invited Bethany to live with them again and she said she wanted to do it. By this time, they had two boys, ages 4 and 1.

Bethany had just turned 14 when she returned to her dad's home and she began a new school year a month later. At first, the only problems that Karen and Jon had were manageable: some missed schoolwork and a bit of backtalk, but nothing serious. All that changed as she got more comfortable in the new environment and made new friends. She started sneaking out at night, despite protests from her best friend that what she was doing was "stupid." But her BFF didn't prevail; instead Bethany's other pals converted her to the "dark side." They all thought sneaking out and even stealing money from parents was okay.

No matter how wild she was with her friends, though, she showed a sweet and playful side to her little stepsiblings.

Even though Bethany was intelligent, she was getting F's in school. It wasn't that she flunked tests or got the homework wrong: She rarely turned work in to her teachers. She had a string of zeroes in most classes.

Karen and Jon took her to a counselor; that made no difference. They sat her down for talks; their caring and concern didn't seem to sink in. They consciously avoided yelling and threatening—precisely what the biological mom did when things went wrong. They coordinated their approach of evenness, firmness, and support.

"Evenness" and "firmness" can have a positive impact as long as they are in the context of empathetic interaction. When regimentation supersedes compassion, a preteen or teen may rebel and, as Bethany told the psychiatrist, come to believe that "No one understands me."

They knew they had to get to the bottom of the problem. They pondered the question—with and without the help of counseling—"why is this happening?" They posed the question directly to Bethany and the default coping mechanism she had developed over the course of years became obvious. She played the blame game by lying. Her responses on why such an intelligent girl would do so badly in school yielded these responses:

"That teacher doesn't explain things well."

"That teacher is boring. No one learns anything from him."

"That teacher's sick all the time, so we have subs."

She was a bad liar, even though she was an inveterate one. Good liars know they should never tell tales that involve other people. Third-party documentation of the false assertion just isn't there. But Bethany plowed on, calling teachers who were heroes to other students, "awful" and "lame."

None of this gets to the heart of the question, "Why is this happening?" Let's look at what she encountered in both of her parents' households to dig out an answer.

The atmosphere at her mother's house was steeped in bitterness since her parents' divorce. Mom yelled when she wasn't happy with her children's behavior, and in Bethany's mind, the only times her mom didn't yell about something or at someone was when she was at work or asleep.

When she was at her father's house, she felt that Karen tried to help and support her, but she had two little kids that were the priorities in her life. Bethany came last in the order of importance, after her stepsiblings and her dad. And even though she wanted desperately to be daddy's girl, he inadvertently blocked her out when she needed him most. He had a reputation for being a perfectionist as a surgeon—his comeback to that was, "Would you want a surgeon who isn't a perfectionist?"—and he brought that standard home. When Bethany didn't perform well, he wanted to remove himself from the situation. After all, if he were involved too deeply, then some of the "failure" might be his fault!

Bethany did not feel heard or understood in either house. She got defensive and shifted responsibility to the adults around her.

Karen and Jon decided that, rather than call her on the lies, they would offer to help her every night with her work. They would explain things the "bad" teacher didn't explain. They would email a teacher when an assignment wasn't clear. They offered to get her a tutor.

So on top of feeling ignored and misunderstood, now she also felt humiliated and angry. Someone would be looking over her shoulder all the time, checking her work, correcting her mistakes, forcing her to comply with the rules.

The first few times they "helped" with her homework, she pretended to cooperate and to listen, especially to her dad. After several rounds yielding no results, though, her dad got frustrated. She would start crying and the whole session would shut down. Finally, all they heard was "No!" Bethany threw fits. She really didn't want any more talk of homework help and tutors. It wasn't her fault.

After the brunt of the problem hit them, just as the first semester was winding down, Karen and Jon went to a parent-teacher conference where they met all of Bethany's teachers. The teachers were not harshly critical; in fact, they were very understanding. They said if she would just pay attention, they thought they could help her. But this was a progressive school where every kid had an iPad, and they never knew what she was doing on her iPad. Short of standing over her and looking at what was on the screen, they didn't know if she was looking at the websites the rest of the class was reviewing, or taking notes, or playing games.

It was at this point that Karen and Jon needed to have Bethany's back with the teachers. They needed to forge a collaborative alliance with them to help her. Instead, all they did was prove Bethany wrong. They came away from the conference praising the teachers and saying what a shame it was that Bethany didn't appreciate all their efforts.

As Bethany withdrew more and more from her family, she came to the odd conclusion that she was winning. No one could pin down what her problems were and all she knew was that no one was yelling at her anymore and she had a really great place to live with adorable little stepsiblings to love her. Life was sweet, sort of.

Near the beginning of the next school year, after having spent the summer with her mother, she took one more step over line. That fall of her second year with her dad and stepmom, she snuck out one night and stole her dad's car. While driving her friends around the neighborhood, she backed it into a tree. She parked the car in the garage, went upstairs and went to bed.

The next morning as he was about to leave for the hospital at six o'clock, Jon found that his car had a dented bumper and a dangling license plate. Bethany had left a stepladder in the car—the ladder she used to reach her friend's bedroom window and knock on it to wake her up.

Jon's first instinct was to call the police and turn his fifteen-year-old daughter in to the authorities. Karen stopped him: "This is a problem that concerns our home and our child. I can't believe that calling in a bunch of outsiders to help us with discipline is going to be the best thing for her or for us as a family."

Karen had worked with a Restorative Justice program for a time and had a good sense of how Bethany's "crime" might be handled in a productive way. She needed to understand the impact of her actions from her victims' perspectives, to understand the potential consequences of her actions, and to feel safe expressing her own fears, regrets, needs, anger, and so on. She set aside time each day to focus exclusively on Bethany—not her homework or her chores, but her well-being. Her dad took a somewhat more regimented approach by having her look up "vehicular homicide" and "grand theft auto" on the Internet so she understood the consequences of being guilty of either one.

"Jon and I talked through household standards and discipline on a regular basis, but with this one, we really had to be on the same page!" says Karen. "She saw a united front at home in terms of discipline, but she also needed to see the consistency of our mutual support. We were so angry with her that it wasn't easy to do."

Karen was hesitant to leave her children—two and five years old at the time—with Bethany, even though she offered to babysit. She had a nagging concern that her stepdaughter would teach them behaviors that Karen and Jon thought were undesirable. Bethany liked her stepsiblings and would protest: "Trust me!"

They decided that perhaps it was time to trust her since she showed more maturity and open affection with her stepsiblings than with anyone else. Karen and Jon let her babysit a few times and everything was fine. Actually, it was more than fine. She clearly loved the kids and they brought out the best in her.

At Chris's request, Bethany went back to her mother's house for the summer. At the beginning of senior year of high school, she immediately reverted to her disruptive behavior and was completely focused on having fun with her friends. By November, realizing that Karen and Jon weren't going to tolerate the violations of household rules, she asked to go back to her mother's house to finish the school year. The mother was against it. Karen and Jon were against it. Bethany's stepsiblings were against it; they enjoyed her company and cried when they heard she was leaving.

Bethany had hit a brick wall with the adults in her life, so she decided to manipulate her mother into taking her back. She "confessed" that Karen had inflicted harsh punishments on her and that it was impossible to please her. The complaints were nonstop, but they never involved Jon; every request to do a chore or disciplinary action was linked to Karen.

So, after yelling at Karen one last time for interfering in her parenting, Chris brought Bethany back to California.

Bethany somehow managed to graduate from high school that year and still lives with her mother a year later. She has a part-time job and is dating a man in his late-twenties—ten years older than she is. College is not a reasonable goal, mostly because she squeaked by in high school and never bothered to take college entrance exams. Chris sees this as a huge disappointment since she has a master's degree in business. Jon recognized this as somewhat predictable and keeps visiting the home in Temecula once a month to try to show support and to mentor her if possible.

Chris does love her children, but they get mixed messages on just about everything. Jon is only there one weekend a month, so they never feel as though they are a priority to him. All three girls tell stories with "omissions and distortions," so lying has become a habit as much as a tool of manipulation for them.

People who lie habitually literally have different brains from the rest of us, according to brain-scan research done at the University of Southern California. The question remains: Were they born that way, or did they rewire the neural pathways related to lying based on their life experiences? The latter would suggest that parenting that does not create a safe haven for kids to express their thoughts and emotions honestly could be considered high-risk in terms of the mental health of children.

Yaling Yang, a psychologist at USC, used fMRI with her test subjects, a combination of documented pathological liars and non-liars. The liars showed 23 to 36 percent more white matter than the non-liars. This is the part of the brain that's associated with storytelling. It's related to personality, attunement to other people, planning complex cognitive behavior, and decision making. The more white matter a person has, the more adept she is at weaving tales. That's very useful if the person is a novelist, but not so great if she's a teenager moving in and out of trouble in school and trying to manipulate a boyfriend into living happily ever after with her. Yang has a hypothesis about what happens that may shock some parents: "It is conceivable that excessive lying repeatedly activates the prefrontal circuit underlying lying, resulting in permanent changes in brain morphology."[1]

Regardless of her word choice of "permanent," the message to all involved in a situation like this is, "Don't give up." The human brain has a stunning capacity for change called "neuroplasticity," which means that it can change physically, functionally, and chemically throughout a person's life.

Continued, steady influence from securely attached people can effect life-changing transformations for someone like Bethany. And even though Bethany blamed Karen for things she never did, she's not delusional. She knows that Karen loves her and tried her best to help her. The secure influences in Bethany's life can still help her change and mature.

STORY B

Shelly—central figure in the story; in the third generation of four involved in the blended families; stepmom to two, but has never functioned as a parental figure; a professional interventionist and counselor

Bill—Shelly's father; avoidant husband, but evolved into a secure parent and secure partner

Millie—Shelly's mother; anxious attachment style with everyone

Cathy—Shelly' s stepmother; secure parenting style

Kevin—Shelly's younger brother; secure parenting style

Ben—Shelly's third husband; avoidant husband and father, but evolved into a secure partner and parent

Ashley—Shelly's stepdaughter; chaotic attachment style, but evolving toward more secure style as a parent

Brad—Shelly's stepson; avoidant attachment style, but evolving toward a more secure style as a parent

Central challenge—Insecure relationships, trauma, and predispositions to addiction have conspired to undermine the happiness of multiple generations

"In my life, the story of blended families is the story of multigenerational trauma. People came together to get on with the business of family and never had a chance to heal." This is how the interview with Shelly began. Shelly has unusually keen insights about the blends in her life because she holds a master's degree in psychology and certifications in addiction intervention and family counseling.

Multigenerational trauma is a common story, unfortunately. Death, divorce, and abandonment can cause blends to occur. If a blend is stable, there is a possibility that the initial trauma won't have ripple effects through subsequent generations. That isn't what happens in many cases, though. What we've seen is that hasty unions "for the sake of the children" or perhaps out of a desperate desire for companionship lead to one more unstable family situation. The children who grow up in that home have a shaky foundation for going forward in their own lives. And on it goes.

This story begins with a sense of doom and gloom, but due to some secure stepparenting in conjunction with parenting that evolved toward secure, some very messy family situations turned around and the effect is now being felt in the third and fourth generations.

It was the early 1940s and Bill was sixteen years old. His father died suddenly of heart failure and, almost as suddenly, his mother remarried her deceased sister's husband. The family instantly became a group of seven that included Bill's two younger sisters and his uncle's two children. It was an uncomfortable, forced coexistence that involved politeness and distance between the stepsiblings.

In marrying Millie when he was in his mid-twenties, Bill was essentially replicating one of the worst parts of his own upbringing. Like his mother, Millie was an anxious woman in desperate need of affirmation and affection. They had two children, Shelly and Kevin. When Shelly was 11 and Kevin was nearly 8, their parents divorced.

Millie moved with her children to a small town a few miles from their previous home, but that was far enough for them to have to change schools. It was one of many significant disruptions. Millie teetered between severe depression and rage because Bill soon married Cathy. She told her young children that their father had cheated on her with Cathy; so Cathy was a whore and her two children were little devils. Although she had to allow Shelly and Kevin to visit their father's home, if they were even one minute late coming back after the visit, they were grounded for a week and screamed at. Millie was always asking questions about their stepmother and trying to build evidence with her children to prove that their father was stupid for divorcing her and marrying Cathy.

The severity of Millie's depression did not become clear until she attempted suicide. But when Burt, the man she fell "over the moon" in love with, entered her life, the depression eased a great deal. However, her happiness was short-lived. Burt was already married.

Shelly remembers her little brother saying, "If you marry Burt, it's okay with me." The simple sentiment expressed in that statement shocked her into breaking off the relationship. Shelly knew that Burt was married because her mother had used her as a confidante, but Kevin had no idea.

Millie snapped after the breakup. She got in her car and drove off, leaving Shelly and Kevin to fend for themselves for a couple of days, until they notified their dad, who immediately came for them and moved them into his house.

Months later, Millie turned up in a mental hospital 900 miles away. She had suffered a dissociative fugue, which in her case involved partial amnesia about her recent past. In the book *The Wandering Mind*, which Maryann wrote with psychiatrist John Biever, they describe the condition as follows:

A person with dissociative fugue (also known as a psychogenic fugue) is fleeing something overwhelming in his life, but that dissociative escape may happen only once as opposed to over and over again. The person will go into a different state of mind, and as part of that journey, will actually physically go someplace else. The person will remain there for a certain period of time—it could be hours or it could be days, months, or years—and do bizarre things; at least they seem bizarre relative to what went before. Most fugues don't involve the formation of a new identity, although they may involve the use of a different name. When different identities do emerge, they are usually characterized by more gregarious and uninhibited traits than those of the core person. During the fugue state, the person won't know where he is or what he's doing. Usually, the state will spontaneously resolve and, when it does, the person may well find himself in a strange place with all of the memories of his regular life intact, but no recollection of what happened in the fugue state. He may even end up in a different city and have no idea how he got there, but he'll know where he came from.[2]

Millie's mind had submerged much more than the memory of the time she was absent. She had gone all the way back in time to 1969, when she was a happily married woman with a new baby girl. It was a safe time in her memory. The amnesia allowed her to have an emotional soft landing after the trauma of both her divorce and the breakup of her passionate relationship with Burt.

The psychiatrist advised Bill to pretend that he and Millie were still married until he could pull her forward in time. She had to be introduced to her own children. She recognized Shelly because of her smile but wondered how she could have grown up so fast. She had no idea who Kevin was since he hadn't been born yet in 1969. Visits from her children and from Bill started to help Millie with her cognitive dissonance. The more she kept asking questions like, "Why are you so old?" the more the amnesiac effects kept dissolving.

Cathy displayed tremendous support and courage and helped all the kids understand the mental illness and to not judge Millie. She stayed steady in her efforts to create a blended family with Bill, her two children, and Shelly and Kevin. What undermined Cathy's and Bill's efforts to provide a consistent, happy home life for these children was an old-fashioned judge.

In 1983, it was still common for judges to give primary custody to a mother, despite the father having more stable circumstances and a demonstrated history of caring for his children better than the mother. The only recourse Bill had was to have everyone show up in court. Shelly remembers the judge asking about her grades when she and Kevin were living with her mother. Both kids were getting straight A's. Did they have enough to eat? Yes. Did they have any trouble getting to school. No. It looked like a case of "Mom's sick and dad is using that to get custody, so he's a bad man."

Despite their desires to stay with their father and Cathy—"We adored her," says Shelly—the two kids had to pack their things and move back with their mother when she was released from the mental health facility. They didn't know it until much later, but Bill had been lobbying the United States Congress with a group of fathers to make it easier for men to gain full parental rights in circumstances where living with dad would be demonstrably better for the kids. This movement has had success in the subsequent decades; however, consider this: There is also a movement to make it easier for stepparents or other nonbiological parent figures to assert custodial rights in cases where the biological parents have not demonstrated their consistent ability to parent well. Although mothers may no longer win by default (this varies from one jurisdiction to another), biological parents do tend to win.

The good news for Shelly and Kevin was that they now had secure, team parenting from their father and stepmother. The bad news was that they had to return to the anxious parenting of their mother on a day-to-day basis.

Within months, Millie eloped with a diabetic, alcoholic man with two teen-agers; all three moved into the home with Millie, Shelly, and Kevin—only to move out again in four months when Millie filed for divorce.

Just after that, Shelly began drinking; she was 16. In spite of her habit, she maintained an A average, status in the National Honor Society, and a strong showing on the volleyball and softball teams. Being home with mom those last two years of high school was filled with anxiety and alcohol took the edge off her anxiety. Millie's emotionally abusive boyfriend moved in their house and Millie had an unplanned pregnancy at the age of 40. At Shelly's graduation, her mother was nine months pregnant and Shelly was marking her 16-month anniversary as a juvenile alcoholic.

Years later, when Shelly was preparing to lead addiction interventions and teach others about multigenerational trauma and patterns, she delved into her own family history. Her mother's mother had been institutionalized for nine months due to an opiate addiction, so Millie had grown up with a mother who was mentally and emotionally very vulnerable and needy. Anxious attachments had dominated mother-daughter relationships in the family for at least two generations.

Shelly's parents started their family with a sense of hopefulness—and per-haps some desperation—that they could create what both of them lacked as kids. Unfortunately, with trauma in both their backgrounds such as addiction, parents' capricious behavior, and other factors leading to emotional abandon-ment and inconsistency, the outcome for each of them wasn't good from an attachment perspective. Anxious attachment—Millie, the "angry pursuer"—and persistent avoidance, which was Bill's style, are how people generally respond to these circumstances.

In the years before she earned her master's degree in psychology and cer-tifications in counseling and intervention, Shelly had been a high-functioning alcoholic. In other words, she had maintained an excellent academic record and, after graduation from college, held a good job with a software develop-ment firm. She had also been married twice; the second time was to a fellow alcoholic she'd met in a bar.

In those years, Bill's marriage to Cathy kept growing stronger. He had confidence as a husband, and provided secure parental influence for his step-children and his son, Kevin, who spent a great deal of time with his dad and stepmother. During that same period, anxious Millie and her abusive husband raised their young son; she was miserable, but felt stuck so she stayed in the marriage.

Shelly knew that her stepmother and her father were a consistently supportive team, so when they arranged an intervention, she felt loved more than judged. She never would have anticipated what happened next, however.

"The families came together because of my alcoholism," says Shelly. The intervention got everyone focused on helping her. Her crisis aroused empathy, compassion, and cooperation.

Shelly agreed to go to treatment. And then the "miracle" occurred: Millie and Cathy drove her to the inpatient program together. As a counselor, Shelly says she commonly sees this kind of behavior:

> I see it all the time that the only things people unite over are illness or some other kind of crisis. Often what happens is that the kids get into trouble—and they don't do this consciously—but they do something that catches the attention of the family. They put something in motion that causes people to come together to focus on them. It's a survival mechanism.

Remember Bethany in Story A running her father's car into a tree? And sneaking out in the middle of the night with her friends? Shelly's insights into her own behavior and the pivotal, family crises related to many children's "bad behavior," suggest that it's certainly possible that stealing the car was Bethany's "cry for help." Her subconscious may have reasoned that this radical action would somehow get the main adults in her life to focus on her feelings for a change. And maybe come together over something.

To a surprising degree, the good effects of coming together over Shelly's alcoholism have lasted. The two families periodically have joint events, mostly centered on holidays. Bill and Cathy remain happy and serve as the core relationship in a healing family.

Committed to her own recovery, Shelly embarked on her new career as an interventionist and counselor. She remained single for nine years and then married Ben, a man with a daughter still in high school and a son who was on his own. Ben had divorced his wife when the children were preteens and they lived with their mother, an alcoholic whose job required traveling more than half the time. The children raised themselves.

Shelly had a chance to see history repeating itself, but this time, she was in a position to do something about it. "History repeating itself" was the emergence of an anxious, angry female and an avoidant, dismissive male from environments characterized by emotional abandonment, addiction, and the trauma of divorce. These were Ben's children, Ashley and Brad, both of whom struggled with substance abuse as young adults.

Ben's daughter Ashley turned to theft to finance her addictions and went to jail. She was shocked and this convinced her she should seek help from her stepmother. Treatment helped, but it didn't help her transform her life until she got pregnant. Shelly wished the circumstances had been more ideal—that Ashley would have spent more time in recovery before becoming a mother—but her course seems to be a good one so far. Ashley remains clean, sober, working, and caring for her toddler with the help of her partner.

She appreciates and accepts the emotional support her father provides and the professional guidance she gets from her stepmother.

Brad's story parallels his sister's so closely that it's eerie. His becoming a parent and husband (in that order) after allowing his stepmother's addiction expertise to affect his life also seem to be moving him in a positive direction.

Ben and Shelly try to remain close to his children and to their children. They are consciously trying to stop the effects of generations of trauma by working toward secure relationships. As far as her title of "stepmom" is concerned, Shelly notes,

> My stepchildren perceive me not as a parental figure, but as someone who has more of a professional role in their lives. I'm an interventionist. A counselor. At the same time, they are genuinely happy I am with their dad because they see how happy he is. In that sense, they recognize me as family.

If all of them continue on the current path, at some point, they will be blended family, and Shelly's "professional role" will probably take a back seat.

STORY C

Heather—mother of two girls; evolved from anxious to secure parenting style

Drew—stepfather of two girls; secure parenting style

Jeff—biological father of two girls; chaotic parenting style with possible antisocial personality disorder

Eva—older daughter; remembers her biological father growing up

Leila—younger daughter; no recollection of her biological father growing up

Central challenge—Biological father decides to reinsert himself in his daughters' lives after absence throughout their childhood

Just as many blended families have had the experience of a crisis drawing people of a family together, others have had the opposite occur: A crisis was the moment when their life together unraveled, at least for a time.

Drew and Heather met at a fitness conference in New York City. He was a single, twenty-seven-year-old and owned a very successful fitness center in Miami. She was 32, going through a divorce, and working as a personal trainer at a private New York club. After losing his job, her husband Jeff walked out on her and left her with their two little girls, ages 1 and 3. All she knew was that he had moved to Boston for a new job.

"Their father was not into the girls at all," says Heather. "They were like props for his resume."

After long-distance dating for a year, Drew and Heather married and she and her daughters moved to Florida. Heather thought through the implications very carefully: "We did all kinds of second-guessing, but ultimately, if the situation is right and the person is right, that's where the focus should be." This is both a typical and a healthy beginning. These are two people who love and respect each other, with the nonparent going into the relationship with his eyes open: There are children involved and they will be with us until they grow up.

Eva remembered her biological father, but Leila was just a baby when he left. Growing up, she didn't remember him at all. As far as she was concerned, Drew was the only father in her life. At the same time, she didn't call him "daddy" or "dad." She called him exactly what her older sister called him—Drewdad.

Sometimes, Eva said she missed her father and couldn't figure out why he left her. Eventually, though, she could understand the difference between someone who happened to be her father and was not around and someone who wasn't her father, but was there for her day after day. Drew made her a priority, but her biological father never did. That realization made her open to having a healthy relationship with Drewdad.

Publicly, both of them referred to him as their father. Most of their friends had no idea that Drew was not their biological father. Heather recalls,

> The girls had such a wonderful childhood with Drew! I can't even believe it really happened. We all got lucky in that respect.
>
> The one thing that seemed to benefit our family unit a lot was that we lived so far apart. He lived in Boston; we lived in Florida. We didn't have a constant interference from someone who wouldn't work with us. Even though we tried, he didn't want to be cooperative. He never did a thing to make the situation work for everybody. It's still that way.

As the girls were growing up, Heather and Drew would occasionally hear from Jeff through a lawyer. He filed several lawsuits in a family court over the course of ten years; these lawsuits are aptly described as "vexatious litigation," meaning that he really just meant to annoy Heather and Drew. Depending on the jurisdiction, myriad accusations could fall into the bucket of "child neglect," for example, so getting a lawyer to take on a case, no matter how frivolous, was relatively easy as long as he had the money to fund the effort.

When the girls were teenagers and all the work of raising them was essentially done, Jeff resurfaced physically. He warned them not to refer to Drew as their father or to call him "dad." He planted ideas in them about spending time with him and described all the things they could do together. The level of control he tried to exercise kept intensifying. The family always had an antagonist in the background, and sometimes he came to the foreground.

Heather noticed that her daughters had nothing of their biological father in them except for genetic influence. Their behavior and values reflected their upbringing by her and Drew. Psychologist and author Daniel A. Hughes (*Building the Bonds of Attachment*) makes it clear that children raised from a very young age by stepparents/adoptive parents can become much more like them in terms of attachment behaviors than their biological parents. The stepparents/adoptive parents can even "undo" the trauma of neglect and even physical harm that biological parents have inflicted on a child by nurturing their capacity for love and fun, and putting healthy discipline in place to engender shame-reduction skill development. He uses the acronym PLACE to remind parental figures of their roadmap to securely attached parenting: Playful, Loving, Accepting, Curious, Empathetic.[3]

Jeff could see that his daughters weren't "his," so he went back to the courts to force them to be "his." He brought a lawsuit regarding Eva's education, asserting that her needs were not being met by the "substandard" public school she was attending. He wanted her to go to boarding school near him in Boston. Despite the fact that Drew was paying for everything in Eva's life—he even paid for the boarding school Jeff insisted she attend—he and Heather decided to let Eva go.

Jeff made sure that no invitation to Eva's graduation went to Drew and Heather. After she received her diploma, she was greeted by her biological father and his parents, who took her to dinner that evening. Drew and Heather took her out for brunch the next day. They let her know how proud they were of her that she had maintained a high average in school and gotten into the college of her choice. Those accomplishments were things they shared with Eva because they raised her. They felt they were far more important than being allowed to attend the graduation, regardless of the symbolism. Nonetheless, taking the high road was not the happiest way to go for them.

Next, Jeff sought a victory with Leila, but it wasn't nearly as easy. She knew that Eva was his favorite; he had barely bothered to acknowledge her most of her life. She made her feelings very clear to him at her high school graduation. When Leila graduated, the small school where she went brought parents directly into the ceremony. As each student got his or her diploma, parents were called onstage to have a photo taken with the graduate and school principal. Heather and Drew knew this was the plan and did not want to make the day awkward for Leila because of her dad; they asked her how she wanted to handle the situation. She said, "He never helped. I don't want his name read. I don't feel comfortable with that." When the names were read, it was Heather and Drew alone who were singled out and invited to come onstage.

Jeff and his parents attended, with his parents seemingly very embarrassed when their son wasn't acknowledged. He was furious. The question that took shape a year later was, "And was he also vengeful?"

Leila's grades put her at the top of her class and she received acceptances to multiple colleges. Drew assured her that he and her mother would find a way to pay the tuition, regardless of where she chose to go. He remembers that, when they talked about it, she said, "You've paid for everything else in my life up to now. Let him pay for college."

Her father agreed on one condition: that she attend a college not far from his current home in Western Massachusetts. It was a school on her list, so she decided to accept. But there was something—or someone, rather—that she wanted to bring with her.

Leila had a long-standing love of horses and had pursued riding and jumping passionately since she was a preteen. She knew that horses weren't cheap. Leila did not take her privilege for granted; she knew the gift of owning and riding a horse had cost her stepfather a great deal. She had also made him and her mother very proud by becoming a grand champion equestrian. When her friends in high school were hanging around the mall and hooking up with guys, Leila was riding.

She asked her mother and stepfather to ship her horse north, so she could continue riding and competing. One Saturday toward the end of her first year in college, she won a competition—another grand championship! That happened at approximately one o'clock in the afternoon. She called her mom and stepfather shortly thereafter to share the good news. Two hours later, she was in a coma.

Jeff didn't notify Drew and Heather until ten o'clock that night, so they couldn't get a flight until the next morning. Leila had been in a one-car accident on a narrow country road and hit a tree.

Suddenly, Jeff seemed to control everyone around him. He was on his home turf, dictating what should happen with his daughter while he sought formal guardianship of her through the local courts. The custodial relationship that Heather had was no longer valid because Leila was 19.

Drew and Heather asked Jeff and the hospital staff concurrently, "What will it take so we can be near her 24/7?" Leila's biological father turned to Drew, standing next to his sobbing wife, and said to him, "Who the f*** does she think she is?"

"Her mother. She has a right to cry," said Drew.

"And who the f*** are you?" he said to Drew.

We note the record of these remarks for two reasons. First, we want to emphasize that a person without capacity for empathy, that is, someone with an antisocial personality disorder, will often use glib remarks and humor inappropriately because he truly doesn't perceive another person's pain.

In the context of Jeff's parenting and throughout this crisis, there is ample evidence that he gives such psychopathic responses. Secondly, his remarks—made in front of hospital staff—were also very likely part of his scheme to get guardianship of his daughter. By suggesting that Leila's mother and stepfather were essentially strangers, he was building a case for how close comparatively he was to her.

Go back for a moment to Story A and the pathological lies associated with Bethany. She was intelligent, and she learned the power of a lie and wasn't reluctant to use it. This is a typical description of someone with antisocial personality disorder—whether the person is aberrant from birth or is the victim of experience.

Jeff's co-conspirator was his wife, who backed him in front of these witnesses in the hospital that "these people" had been absent from Leila's life in recent times and had no business being there.

They saw the horse. And Leila's stepfather and mother made sure she had her own car. Clearly, Drew was successful. They potentially had a lot to gain financially by exercising leverage over the daughter that Jeff had shown no interest in for most of her life.

Over the next couple of weeks, Heather and Drew lived in a hotel near the hospital and spent as much time as they were allowed with Leila. Then one day, they were blocked from entering. Jeff had been effective in getting guardianship and the first things he did were cut them off from communication. They couldn't visit. They couldn't even leave a text on her phone for later because he shut off her phone service. He left them with nothing but a stack of photographs of the accident scene. Time and date stamps indicated that he'd been taking pictures instead of calling them on the day of the crash.

During the six weeks of this ordeal, Drew's father was dying of stomach cancer. He left Heather in Massachusetts to continue the fight to see her daughter and went to Maryland to spend his father's final days with him.

Drew's father had been a prisoner of war for several years, and the experience seemed to help forge a philosophical approach to life. He was a gentle and spiritual man who had found a career late in life as a sculptor. When father and son talked about Leila, Drew's father remarked, "My heart breaks for her mother."

The day before he died, he put his hand on Drew's and said, "It's time for me to go home. That will give her strength." He was talking about Leila.

The next day, Drew watched his father take his last breath. Less than an hour later, his cell phone rang. It was Heather: "Leila woke up!"

The aftereffects of a traumatic brain injury often involve memory loss and there's invariably some level of confusion. Jeff's repeated message to Leila was that her mother and stepfather were not there for her. They stayed in

Florida; they didn't care. These were some of the first things she heard after waking up.

But as she grew stronger and had contact with her mother and Drew, the embedded and long-term memories that often remain after this kind of injury were still there. Talking with her sister, reminiscing about childhood adventures with her family, all triggered recollections of very happy years filled with love and joy.

No matter what he did, her biological father could never take them away. She wanted to go home to mom and Drewdad.

SLIGHTLY UNCONVENTIONAL BLENDS
THAT WORKED . . . AND WHY

Danny, Lisa, three girls, and a boy

Danny's wife died, leaving him with three girls, ages 4, 6, and 10. He had a house in suburban Washington, DC, with a small guest wing that he'd built for his in-laws to reside in. With his wife gone, they would not be moving in. He posted an ad for a housemate and Lisa responded. The only problem, she explained during the interview, was that she was a single mom who came with a nine-year-old son. Danny and the girls liked Lisa and Jake; the ten-year-old already knew him from school. "It's okay with us, Dad," the girls agreed.

The first week they were in the house, Lisa started cooking dinner for everyone. She had a job with the Department of Labor and got off work at five o'clock every day, whereas Danny's work as a tax attorney often kept him at the office late.

There were no sparks between Danny and Lisa. They didn't find each other particularly attractive, although they became friends almost immediately and trusted each other with the kids. After two years of living under the same roof and dating other people, they realized that they enjoyed each other's company more than going out with other people. Among other things they liked doing together, he would relax late at night by playing his guitar and she would sing along.

At some point, about three years into the arrangement, Lisa moved out of the guest wing and into Danny's room. They saw no reason to get married, but their enjoyment of and appreciation for each other grew through the years. They also shared a secure style of parenting.

The kids could not have been happier. In fact, they wondered why it took Danny and Lisa so long to figure out what they thought was an obvious match.

A 2014 study done by researchers for Canada's National Bureau of Economic Research concluded that "well-being effects of marriage are about twice as large for those whose spouse is also their best friend."[4] The data came from multinational sources, including the British Household Panel Survey and the Gallup World Poll. Although Danny and Lisa chose not to marry, their exclusive partnership reflected the same level of commitment to each other and to their children as a married couple—or at least as a married couple would hope to have.

Mark, Dave, Janet, and a son

Dave had served in the Army for fifteen years before he admitted to himself and his wife, Janet, that he was homosexual. Their son was eight years old at the time of their amicable divorce.

Mark worked as an architect at the Department of Veterans Affairs (VA) and met Dave in a hallway when he'd come on VA one morning on a matter related to his service. It was six months after Dave's divorce. The attraction was strong; in a matter of a few minutes, they decided to have lunch the next day.

Having gone through comparable struggles with his sexuality, Mark had a lot of empathy for Dave. He also knew what it felt like to lose someone important: His life partner had died of AIDS. Mark had sensitivity to Dave's sense of loss over Janet and the prospect of having limited contact with his son.

They moved in together three months later. Six years after that, they married; it was a time before the Supreme Court's decision on marriage equality, so they married as soon as the District of Columbia allowed them to do so. Janet served as a witness; Dave's son, Pat, served as best man.

Healthy co-parenting characterized this blended family. Dave, Janet, and Mark supported Pat in his schoolwork, came to his basketball games, and had holidays as a family. Pat met Mark's friends from work and filled in as short-stop on the VA architects' softball team when they were one player short.

Janet's and Dave's divorce was no one's fault. Respect for family, and the choices needed to create a family, dominated the interaction. The couple at the center of this blend—technically speaking—was Mark and Dave. But this was really a three-way, core unit. Janet always had a continuing role in co-parenting, so the three of them made Pat's sense of family complete.

Paul, Bunny, Jack, Anna, Sylvie, Jen, and Alex

Paul's biological father had been uncomfortable with his wife's wealth from the beginning. Bunny had inherited an immense fortune. She also handled it gracefully and made no attempt to use it as leverage in her marriage. But Paul's father felt emasculated by her money. He had two goals when they got married: Get her pregnant and make a lot of money. It was a case of "That'll show them I belong with her!"

He succeeded in both with unfortunate consequences. Working long hours to achieve his financial goals, he rarely spent time with his son and wife. When Paul was five, Bunny filed for divorce. She had met Jack, a Wall Street broker, and wanted to marry him. Paul's father did not contest. He quickly accepted a promotion that required him to move to London; he left his family behind except for calling Paul on his birthday and holidays.

Bunny moved with her son, as well as her housekeeper and nanny—Anna and Sylvie, respectively—to New York City from Philadelphia. And on most weekends her favorite niece, sixteen-year-old Jen, took the train up to be with Aunt Bunny. Jack went from bachelorhood and a studio loft to an Upper East Side, five-bedroom penthouse apartment.

During her years with an absentee husband, Bunny had developed a close relationship with Anna and Sylvie, and Jen's weekend visits got her out of the house to shop and see movies. As soon as everyone moved to New York, however, relationships shifted. Bunny and Jack sailed on some weekends, went to the theater on others, and liked to try new restaurants. Jen sometimes went along, but not having Aunt Bunny all to herself, she cut back on her visits within a couple of months. A year later, Alex was born; "Jen's room" became a nursery.

Within the next year, Anna began taking the train back to Philadelphia more often and soon took another position as a live-in with a family there. Sylvie stayed on for another four years, but she and Bunny had lost the intimate conversational connection they had before she married Jack.

The blend evolved into the closely knit foursome of Bunny, Jack, Paul, and Alex. The extra bedrooms came in handy when Jack decided he needed a study and Paul wanted a guest room available for his buddies.

While Bunny had become anxious and fearful during her first marriage, she moved steadily toward a more secure attachment style with Jack. And even though Paul had always felt safe and cared for by his mother and Sylvie, the absence of his father had affected him. He tended to withdraw whenever there was difficult moment in the household. His mother's marriage to Jack made him feel as though he was part of a real family—a family that, for him, included Sylvie. They stayed in touch; she took other positions in Manhattan so she was never far away. Anna, too, still exchanges gifts and cards with the family.

The key to the success of the blend was always the partnership of Bunny and Jack. They focused on each other, not getting sidetracked with the fact that she had great wealth, and as a result, were able to create a loving, supportive home for Paul and Alex. But it was also a home where it became quite clear who belonged to the family and who was invited to participate in it.

Paul always referred to Jack by his name, but in many ways, he saw him as his father. Jack mentored him and was a good role model. He had his back during tough times in school and taught him how to be a good first mate—and later, captain—on the family sailboat. When Paul graduated from college, with both Jack and his biological father present, he showed his dad a lot of affection. Bunny saw it as a bit ironic, considering that the man who helped nurture that emotional maturity was Jack. It was one more thing she celebrated that day.

POINTS TO CONSIDER

A blended family has life because of the couple that joined together to create the new family. Sometimes the path to a blend is circuitous and unusual, of course. Children put a lot of unpredictable elements in play so the family keeps on blending. Everyone has to come together to sustain the blend, and that can take a long time. The average (supposedly) is seven years, but that's just an average. Keep at it, being conscious of what it takes to express and feel secure attachments. A good guide is the one mentioned in the above story that psychologist Dan Hughes provided: Practice PLACE, that is, be

Playful
Loving
Accepting
Curious
Empathetic

NOTES

1. Yaling Yang, Adrian Raine, Katherine L. Narr, Todd Lencz, Lori Lacasse, Patrick Colletti, Arthur W. Toga. "Localisation of increased prefrontal white matter in pathological liars," *The British Journal of Psychiatry* 190 (2) January 2007: 174–175; doi: 10.1192/bjp.bp.106.025056.

2. John A. Biever and Maryann Karinch, The *Wandering Mind*, Rowman & Littlefield, 2010, p. 32.

3. Daniel A. Hughes, *Building the Bonds of Attachment*, Jason Aronson, Inc, 1998; p. 302.

4. John F. Helliwell, Shawn Grover, "How's Life at Home? New Evidence on Marriage and the Set Point for Happiness," National Bureau of Economic Research, NBER Working Paper No. 20794; Issued in December 2014; http://www.nber.org/papers/w20794.

Chapter 12

Advice from the Front Line—Blending DOs and DON'Ts

Individuals and couples we interviewed, as well as survey participants who volunteered narrative responses, offered a plethora of "do this; don't do that" tips. We took those we heard relatively often and then integrated them with Trevor's insights from an attachment perspective as well as with comments from other experts that either supported or refuted the advice. This chapter is the resulting DOs and DON'Ts, with a focus on the big challenges facing a couple *as a couple* in a blended family as well as *parents/stepparents* in a blended family.

DOS AND DON'TS FOR COUPLES

- DO learn from your family history how the dynamics of your family of origin shaped your attachment style.

  Forty percent of the children born in the late 1970s experienced their families breaking up. The numbers have risen since then, but it's likely that many people reading this book fall into that 40 percent of Generation Xers (born 1975–1985) with divorced parents. If your parents were divorced, then your family situation gave you a greater chance of divorcing, with divorce being a likely reason you are now in a blended family. In *Understanding the Divorce Cycle: The Children of Divorce in their Own Marriages*, sociologist Nicholas H. Wolfinger explains why children whose parents divorce are more likely to divorce than people whose parents' marriage remained intact. He doesn't conclude that it's merely conflicts and incompatibilities that are key factors, but rather the lessons learned about marital commitment.[1] "Commitment issues" along with "irreconcilable differences" are concepts that came to the fore of the divorce discussion after 1969, when Governor Ronald Reagan of California signed the nation's first no-fault divorce bill. Prior to that, one of the reasons why the divorce rate was much lower—about 11 percent in the 1950s—is that divorce required pointing fingers and laying blame. Churches also played a bigger role in "mandating" that marriages stay together than they did as the twentieth century came to a close.

Wolfinger offers some other interesting study results that have been quoted by others as a way of demonstrating the long-term devastation of divorce. We give them to you because they capture statistically how difficult it is to hold households together in an era of no-fault divorce—but we offer them with a caveat: These numbers do not suggest a *fait accompli* in terms of your marriage and family. The whole point of sharing guidance from experts and insights from those in happy blends is to shine a light on the possibilities for you.

In his book, Wolfinger says that respondents to the General Social Surveys (GSS) "who experienced both parental divorce and remarriage were 91 percent more likely end their own marriages than were people from intact families."[2] The GSS is a national survey conducted annually or biannually with sample sizes of more than 10,000 people; Wolfinger used data over a twenty-year period. He also says that "parental divorce [without remarriage] increases the chances of offspring divorce by at least 40 percent, irrespective of measures of family structure and adjustments for differences between respondents."[3]

Now put the numbers aside and embrace the advantages you have over many other people who are trying to blend families. For starters, having a sense of your own attachment style, as well as how it took shape, means that you know where you've been and where you're headed. You have insights into your strengths and shortcomings as a partner and as a parent. You self-awareness is the first, giant step to beating the odds.

- ○ DON'T blame your parents or your partner's parents for any challenges you might be having. As a couple, try to move toward more secure attachment with each other; keep the focus on your union as the core of the blended family.
- DO listen at least as much as you talk with your partner. Try to listen with focus and full attention on your partner. Even in ordinary "how was your day, dear" conversations, research has shown that lack of listening both signals, and contributes to, relationship problems.

John Gottman is an award-winning psychologist who is known globally for his work on marital stability and divorce. One of his studies resulted in a model that attempted to predict when a couple will divorce over a fourteen-year period. The model proved to be accurate 93 percent of the time!

Although the big element that helped him reliably predict divorce was the pursuer-withdrawer style of interaction—one partner has an anxious attachment style and pursues, while the other has an avoidant attachment style and responds by withdrawing—listening was an important element, too:

It was interesting that divorce prediction was possible by examining affect even during the events-of-the-day conversation. This was the first interaction the couple had following their reunion after 8 hours of separation. Upon first examination, this conversation appears to be a fairly neutral (and, according to most of our coders, even a boring) conversation for almost all couples. We were not surprised that affect during this conversation had predictive power for ascertaining the future stability of the marriage.

In a careful viewing of the videotapes, we noticed that there were critical moments during the events-of-the-day conversation that could be called either "requited" or "unrequited" interest and excitement. For example, in one couple, the wife reported excitedly about something their young son had done that day, but she was met with her husband's disinterest. After a time of talking about errands that needed doing, he talked excitedly about something important that happened to him that day at work, but she responded with disinterest and irritation. No doubt this kind of interaction pattern carried over into the rest of their interaction, forming a pattern for "turning away" from one another.[4]

○ DON'T act like what you have to say is more important that what your partner has to share with you. Sure, if your son breaks his arm, that's important news, but giving relatively trivial problems too much emotion and time is how some people make a desperate play for attention. Focus on your partner when he or she is talking and, hopefully, that person will display the same respect for you.

• DO acknowledge your partner when he or she makes a valid point in a discussion, even if you don't agree with it. Otherwise, your response could create a confrontational atmosphere—and that will poison attempts to continue your conversation about the topic.

John Gottman identified what he calls the Four Horsemen, which are four potentially devastating communication styles for a couple. They are criticism, contempt, defensiveness, and stonewalling and they are most likely to surface in any interaction where the two members of the couple don't agree on something. The Gottman Relationship Blog featured a quiz one day to help readers assess the presence of these four styles in their relationship. With permission of The Gottman Institute, we are offering you the quiz so you can ascertain how prominent the Four Horsemen might be in the communication you have with your partner. Read each statement, and then answer "true" or "false."

When we discuss our relationship issues:

1. I feel attacked or criticized when we talk about our disagreements.
2. I usually feel like my personality is being assaulted.
3. In our disputes, at times, I don't even feel like my partner likes me much.
4. I have to defend myself because the charges against me are so unfair.
5. I often feel unappreciated by my partner.
6. My feelings and intentions are often misunderstood.
7. I'm not appreciated for all the good I do in this relationship.
8. I often just want to leave the scene of arguments.
9. I get disgusted by all the negativity between us.
10. I feel insulted by my partner at times.
11. I sometimes just clam up and become quiet.
12. I can get mean and insulting in our disputes.
13. I basically feel disrespected.
14. Many of our issues are just not my problem.
15. The way we talk makes me want to withdraw from the whole relationship.
16. I think to myself, "Who needs all this conflict?"
17. My partner never really changes.
18. Our problems have made me feel desperate at times.
19. My partner doesn't face issues responsibly and maturely.
20. I try to point out flaws in my partner's personality that need improvement.
21. I feel explosive and out of control about issues at times.
22. My partner uses phrases like "You always or "You never" when complaining.
23. I often get the blame for what are really our shared problems.
24. I don't have a lot of respect for my partner's position on our basic issues.
25. My partner can be quite selfish and self-centered.
26. I feel disgusted by some of my partner's attitudes.
27. My partner gets far too emotional.
28. Small issues often escalate out of proportion.
29. Arguments seem to come out of nowhere.
30. My partner's feelings get hurt too easily.[5]

- There is no key associated with this quiz, so there is no high score or low score. If your responses concern you, refer to the subsequent four DOs in this section and try to avoid the DON'Ts. The DOs reflect insights we heard from interviewees, but they are structured to reflect Gottman's guidance on the Four Horsemen.

- ○ DON'T talk to your partner as though you are always right. "Being right" has got to be a shared experience, so listen carefully so the two of you can find common ground.
- DO express the emotion you're feeling when your partner criticizes you. If the biological father of your stepson says something like, "You can be mean to Robbie—I heard you yell at him yesterday!"—state how you feel in a straightforward way. "I feel insecure about being a parent to him. Please understand that I am trying to do my best and I need you to work with me on this."
  - ○ DON'T lash out. Fight the urge to counter with a criticism like "You yell at him, too, when he throws his backpack down the stairs!"
- DO bite your tongue if have the urge to flavor your conversation with disdain. Quick-witted people tend to be very skilled at this; they think of the "right" retort when they're in the heat of the moment. (The rest of us think about that sharp comeback two days later—thank goodness!)

Journalist Anderson Cooper interviewed Gottman about his Four Horsemen concept and had this to say about the expression of contempt for a partner: "I'd never heard that showing contempt for somebody else—one partner in a relationship showing contempt—really has a physical effect, that it actually can affect your immune system."[6] This is a reality that drove the lessons we offered in *Forging Healthy Connections*:

> In biochemical terms, when we are relaxed and feeling safe our bodies make more feel-good hormones, like oxytocin and opiates. We are predisposed to be healthier. When we're stressed, under some kind of physical or psychological threat, we make hormones that wear down our immune system.[7]

- ○ DON'T take the clever path to conversation. In other words, don't enjoy the sound of your own wit so much that you sacrifice real conversation just to insert a zinger into the dialogue. Get a journal; write it down and use it in your novel.
- DO step up to a tough discussion with straightforward responses and not a bunch of excuses. Getting defensive and portraying yourself as a victim will either create, or help to create, an imbalance in the interaction. It's perfectly natural to feel defensive when your partner blames you for something that is not your fault, but try not to act on that feeling. Exercising this kind of restraint, even when it comes to little things, will boost the honesty level of your conversations. For example, if your partner says, "I asked you to do that one little thing and you didn't do it!" you might respond with a simple "I'm sorry; I forgot" instead of an excuse about why you forgot.

○ DON'T turn the tables when you feel defensive. In response to "I asked you to do that one little thing and you didn't do it!" you do not want to say, "You weren't as busy as I was so why didn't you do it yourself?"

• DO stay engaged in the interaction, even when you find it somewhat uncomfortable. It's horrible to be the partner who is trying to explain feelings and make progress in a conversation, only to have the other person physically or figuratively leave the room. Gottman calls this latter behavior "stonewalling," and he offers the following guidance to the partner who is the victim of this kind of avoidance: "The first part of the antidote to experiencing this extreme unpleasantness is to STOP. The second step is to practice physiological self-soothing."[8]

The advice to "stop" involves verbalizing the fact that you feel overwhelmed and agitated; ask for a break to calm down. When emotions run high, the cognitive part of your brain functions poorly, or not at all. That's no time to try to have a constructive conversation, so take twenty to thirty minutes to get your "head" back. During that break, self-soothing actions are necessarily things that take you away from the heated interaction. Go for a walk around the block, or watch twenty minutes of a sitcom on TV.

○ DON'T push your stonewalling partner to reengage when you sense that total withdrawal from the discussion. Acknowledge that the conversation needs to continue, but that this clearly isn't the time to do it.

• DO give benefit-of-the-doubt behavior precedence over quick judgment. This is innately hard for analytical people to do because, in many cases, their careers are built on their ability to calculate and judge quickly. Remember that this is your partner and your family you are dealing with now, and not colleagues, staff, or vendors. Train yourself to have a nonjudgmental first response at home: Be kind and generous with your family. Relationships are not transactional. They are based on emotional bonds.

○ DON'T resort to *quid pro quo* when you think you're right. That is, you've already made a judgment that your partner has made a mistake and you won't forgive him unless and until he forgives a mistake you've made in the past. Linking "mistakes" over time, and dredging them up whenever there is a disagreement, is insecure and selfish.

• DO have firm agreement on money issues. From household expenses to allowances for biological and stepchildren to estate planning, make sure that you and your partner don't surprise each other. An example of a surprise would be a biological child getting more money on the side than the stepsiblings. Naturally, if a child get sick or needs a little extra cash to go to the prom, exceptions can be made—but they should be made in agreement. Many therapists, as well as money managers, agree with financial advisor and TV host Suze Orman when she says, "For my money, not being on the same page financially is a sure ticket to marital discord, if not divorce."[9] Orman offers couples three "money vows" so that couples can add what she calls "financial intimacy" to their emotional intimacy:

1. No matter who earns what, we will equally share all money decisions.
2. We will be financially intimate and still retain our own financial identities.
3. We love each other so much, we will have a prenup agreement.[10]

- ○ DON'T use lack of a child support payment by an ex as evidence that you or your children are victims, or conversely, to use it as leverage that "you're better than that." Just deal with the situation jointly, as though you had to get your house patched because of a roof leak. You are partners; it's a joint problem that demands a joint solution.
- ○ DON'T be arbitrary in estate planning. When your family includes biological and nonbiological children, one type of child is not better than another. Fairness and coordination with your partner must undergird the decisions you make, and we strongly recommend going to an investment professional who specializes in blended families for the best help.

- DO behave in a trustworthy manner with your partner; this will help you boost the level of trust in your relationship. This is the behavior of someone with a secure attachment style. Questions or statements that originate in suspicion or jealousy trigger resentment. If you think you have a reason to be suspicious or jealous—if you observe behaviors that shake your trust—go to couple's counseling. With a skilled therapist guiding the conversation, you are more likely to find out where you stand with each other emotionally without either party flying into a rage.
  - ○ DON'T let jealousy about your partner's ex-spouse poison your relationship. The two of you are together now for a reason; your partner split with the ex for a reason.
  - ○ DON'T let jealousy about your ex's new partner drive your attention away from your relationship. Comparing yourself to the "new man" or "new woman" does no one any good; you have your own relationship that requires your focus, so take your mind off your ex's. During our interviews, one woman told us about a friend of hers whose wealthy ex-husband had a string of beautiful young girlfriends after he divorced her. This woman would tell her daughters to take pictures, when they visited their father, of their father's girlfriends secretly with their smartphones! She got the shock of her life—and put her children in an extremely awkward position—when one of the photos showed that the latest girlfriend was pregnant.

Your need to know something about your ex's new partner should be limited to how it might affect your children when they are under the same roof with that person. That issue relates to the DOs and DONTs of parenting, however, and not to your relationship with your partner.

- DO learn how to negotiate with your partner. Since it's a given that you won't always agree on the best ways to manage your blended household, you may want to rely on some tips from Roger Fisher and Daniel Shapiro of the Harvard Negotiation Project. The project itself aims to improve the theory and practice of conflict resolutions, but Fisher and Shapiro focused their work within it on the emotional aspects of negotiation.

Their approach involves partners focusing on "core concerns." They list these five as the issues that arouse the emotions you feel during a negotiation with your partner:

1. Appreciation
   - Ignored when your thoughts, feelings, or actions are devalued.
   - Met when your thoughts, feelings, or actions are acknowledged.
2. Affiliation
   - Ignored when you are treated as an adversary and kept at a distance.
   - Met when you are treated as a partner.
3. Autonomy
   - Ignored when your freedom to make your own decisions is impinged upon.
   - Met when others respect your freedom to decide important matters.
4. Status
   - Ignored when your relative standing is treated as inferior to the other.
   - Met when you are given equal standing and recognition.
5. Role
   - Ignored when others plays the role of an adversary (me vs. you).
   - Met when others play the role of an ally.[11]

Take a moment to think about the last time you negotiated with your partner, and ask yourself if your needs were met in the five areas listed. If not, what happened or what was said that made you feel the need was ignored? Now turn the question around: What might you have said or done that left that need unfulfilled for your partner?

- DON'T act like you're a hostage negotiator. Someone in that position is always calculating what the other person has to lose, and always trying to convince the other person that he or she is winning. It's artful manipulation, which is not what you want to do at home.
- DO disengage yourself from your ex. You are divorced for a reason, so hanging out together, especially when you have a new partner, is generally

not a good idea. We know one couple that was in the floral design business together and kept working together even after the divorce. His new spouse was justifiably concerned about the long hours that he continued to spend with his ex. She knew that their divorce had been caused by his running around with other women; she was one of the other women. "If he ran around with me when he was with her, will he run around with her while he's with me?" she wondered. The marriage only pulled together after the ex-spouse remarried and her new husband bought out the ex.

- ○ DON'T forget why you are no longer with the other biological parent of your children. The reason doesn't have to haunt you, but it needs to remain a reality in your life.
- • DO be aware of your physical and emotional processing in the moment. The more self-aware you are, the better you can respond to most things with love and kindness and not dismissal or annoyance. One interview with a mom led to a discussion about empathy and what it means. She recalled the main points—tap into your own feelings and truly understand what he's going through and not just feel sorry for him—and that made a big difference in how she processed the distress of her partner after he heard he *might* get laid off. She said her normal reaction would have been, "Well it hasn't happened yet, so don't worry." Instead, she locked into his anxiety and met it with compassion. She'd been fired once, so she could relate to how threatened and beaten down he felt. Just knowing that she connected with his concerns gave him strength.
  - ○ DON'T make your own story dominant when your partner is experiencing pain or anxiety. Communicate that you can relate his or her emotion, but don't shift the conversation to something that you went through that was worse or more dramatic.
- • DO express appreciation to your partner (and to your children). Earlier in the book, we told the story of a stepmom who helped her stepdaughter through a lot of issues, but the biological father never expressed his gratitude. She didn't resent it, but she made it clear that it would have meant a lot to her to hear a simple "Thank you."
  - ○ DON'T take it for granted that your partner knows how you feel. Express appreciation and tender feelings on a regular basis. In her practice, Trevor has seen that the lack of such communication causes damage over time.
- • DO be aware that, as part of a couple, you are always asking two questions: (1) Are you there for me? (Do you have my back?) and (2) Am I important to you? (Am I your priority and do you really know me?) If something is causing distance in a couple, it is almost always rooted in one of those questions.
  - ○ DON'T avoid the conversation you need to have with your partner if the answer to one of the questions is "No." Ideally, seek counseling with a

clinician who does EFT because these questions will be familiar ones to him or her. They come out of the work of Sue Johnson, a cofounder of EFT.

DOS AND DON'TS FOR PARENTS/STEPPARENTS

In Chapter 3, we introduced some DON'Ts from interviewees regarding parenting and stepparenting and explained their importance to healthy communication in a blended family. To recap, we noted:

• DON'T use your children as conduits of information between you and an ex.
• DON'T pump your kids for information about an ex.
• DON'T speak ill about an ex in front of that person's child.
• DON'T expose the kids to conversations about finances and other private matters pertaining strictly to your household.

In this chapter, we provide a few more DON'Ts, but the focus is on the DOs and why they help you make progress in blending.

• DO try to do everything possible to co-parent with an ex. You want to do everything you can to give your children a sense of security and belonging. Your child feels as though he's respected and cared for when both biological parents are coordinated on schedules, school issues, and other matters related to his well-being. He'll be better able to cope with the effects of the divorce, and is likely to be more open to a stepparent, if he feels that both biological parents have his back.
    This kind of co-parenting includes continued contact with your former in-laws; cousins, aunts, and uncles are all part of that family group. As long as the relationship between your children and your ex's relatives was healthy before, it would benefit the kids if they maintain that connection.
    ◦ DON'T bully an ex into co-parenting; don't use guilt trips to get an ex into participating in a child's life. In some cases, no matter what you do, interest in the kids might wane over time, or not be there at all. They would be far better off receiving support and attention from an interested stepparent than a disinterested biological parent.
    ◦ DON'T make your kids feel guilty about enjoying their time with your ex, the ex's new partner, and step- and half-siblings in the other household. In any joint custody arrangement, the kids will be splitting their time between households, and that often means two blended

households. The mix of expectations related to behavior, meals and mealtimes, and activities, among other things, could be dramatically different. Don't make it more stressful for your kids by enforcing a "be back by five o'clock on Sunday or your grounded" approach to co-parenting or by not letting them tell you the fun things they did over the weekend.

- DO establish strong boundaries if you have a contentious relationship with an ex. There is no reason to subject yourself, your children, partner, or stepchildren to an ex's abusive, vengeful, or disgusting behavior. At the same time, with boundaries in place, even a horrible ex can be given an opportunity to spend some quality time with his or her child. One person we interviewed described criminal behavior of an ex that involved forgery and fraud. Another said that her ex had become a cocaine addict. Even these extremes of bad behavior are not absolute reasons to cut off all ties between the ex and that person's biological children, but they are reasons to orchestrate the contact so that the child is protected—both from lies and from physical danger.
  - DON'T punish your children for your ex's inappropriate or illegal behavior. Blocking all contact between parent and child will not help the child develop some perspective on what's happened in his family. And instead of having some compassion for the parent who has made mistakes, he's likely to judge and condemn that parent—and there's something innately unhealthy in carrying that attitude through life.
- DO restrain yourself in making comparisons between your biological child, or your partner's biological child, and an absent parent.

  Your child has a genetic bond to both you and your ex. She may look like your ex, talk like your ex, and have mannerisms that remind you of your ex—just don't focus on the similarities unless it involves a distinct positive. It's fine to tell your daughter that her performance at her piano recital reminded you of her father—"you have your dad's musical gifts"—if the dad is a concert pianist. It's not fine to tell her she's acting "just like her dad" when she leaves the dinner table without excusing herself.

  The same kind of restraint is necessary for a stepparent. You want to help nurture the child's self-esteem by focusing on the gifts her biology gave her, and not make remarks like "I heard your dad had a bad stutter like yours until he was in his mid-twenties."
  - DON'T badmouth the child, either, by telling an ex "she's just like you!"—and not in a good way. In the interests of co-parenting well, keep the comparisons positive to reinforce their connection in a good way.
- DO encourage the child to open up about his problems without blaming the absent parent for them. A child shouldn't feel guilty about bringing

his absent biological parent into a conversation, but steer him away from criticism of your ex or your partner's ex. Help him frame the challenge he's facing and identify solutions without pointing a finger at that person.

- ○ DON'T forbid the child to talk about your ex. As painful as it might be to you to even hear his or her name, as long as the reference doesn't come with rancor toward either one of you, let it stand.
- ○ DON'T tell your children the dirty details of your divorce, or you will provide ammunition for them to use that information against both you and your ex. You want to engender an ability to have compassion and empathy for you and others, but you don't want to do it by telling your children how much your ex hurt you. Your children should not be made to serve as your confidants in matters related to your divorce from their other biological parent.

- • DO support your biological child in developing a relationship with half-siblings. They innately have parts of them in common that give them a foundation for communicating and connecting.
  - ○ DON'T sabotage the relationship between your biological children and those that your ex has with a new partner. If your ex forms a new family that includes children who are biologically related to your child(ren), do not block their attempts to bond. Don't be selfish and assert that your children are betraying you by trying to connect with their half sisters and brothers.

- • DO be honest about your shortcomings as a parent or stepparent, without going into messy details. It's a relief for a kid to hear, "I apologize for being short tempered with you this morning. I was more focused on my presentation at work than what you needed from me for school."

  Mistakes are a learning tool. As long as you admit when you make one and do your best to avoid repeating it, your children and stepchildren will see that mature adults don't beat themselves up every time they aren't perfect. Acknowledging a bad moment or shortcoming and moving on sends a powerful message about the potential we all have to improve.
  - ○ DON'T spill your guts about what a "bad mom" or "bad dad" you think you are. No child wants to hear that his parent or stepparent thinks she's doing a lousy job. And don't spill your guts about the really stupid things you did as a teenager in an effort to bond with your child or stepchild. Save that kind of admission for your friends, or for when your kid is in her 40s.
  - ○ DON'T minimize something serious that you've done when you are talking about it with an older child. If your daughter knows you cheated on her mother and that's what triggered the divorce, then don't insult her or your ex by trying to justify your actions.

- DO get clear with your partner on how you talk about the exes to the kids. If your relationship with your ex is acrimonious, you want your partner to say nothing more than, "Sorry, Derek, but it's best if you ask your mom about why your dad acted like that." On the other hand, if an ex is integrated into the family to some degree, then positive references to a partner's ex are fine: "You're really lucky to have such a kind mom, Isla. She and your dad love you so much."
  - DON'T make assumptions that saying something positive about your partner's ex makes it okay to talk about him or her to the kids. Even saying something nice could confuse the kids, so make sure you and your partner are clear on what kind of references are appropriate.
- DO consider the feelings of the kids when it comes to events like graduations, birthdays, and holidays. In the course of your children's lives, you and your ex will undoubtedly end up at some of the same functions because your children want both of you there. Try to establish the ground rules in advance so that the stepparents involved feel appreciated and included and the exes don't find themselves in awkward situations with photographs or meals. Remember: At events like this, it isn't about you, it's about the child who is graduating or celebrating a birthday. Keep your focus where it belongs.
  - DON'T use events like this as leverage with a child. As a therapist, Trevor has seen this happen many times, particularly with big life events such as graduation from high school and college. One parent will threaten not to attend unless he and his new wife can take the graduate to dinner. The other parent will threaten not to attend unless the graduation party is at her house with her friends. This is a nightmare for a child who should be celebrating one of the greatest moments of his or her young life.
- DO stay involved consistently in your children's and stepchildren's lives while, at the same time, give them autonomy to get away from you. As a reminder, this book is focused on a blended family with 8- to 18-year-olds, so we are talking about ages when kids must have both support and independence. If you are a stepparent, coordinate with the biological parent about what types of responsibilities you can give your stepchild, as well as how far you can go to help with homework, coaching a sport, and so on. Remind each other that you have to let go sometimes!
  - DON'T try to so hard to "make up" for the absence of a biological parent that, as a stepparent, you insert yourself to "help" at every opportunity. You have a responsibility to provide parenting, not to overdo parenting.
  - DON'T try to be cool and follow your stepchild on social media. Follow people your own age.
  - DON'T do things for the child that she can do for herself. If you're a stepmom who grew up in a household where every kid knew how to run

the lawnmower and cut the grass, don't just cut the grass yourself when your stepdaughter says she has no idea how to use the lawnmower. If this is the kind of chore that you and your partner agreed she should do, then teach her how and turn her loose.

○ DON'T minimize a child's struggle with self-image issues. If you are involved on a day-to-day basis, you can see that pimples, last year's clothes, school bullies, and other challenges of life are having a profound effect on how she sees herself. Whether you are a parent or stepparent, get practical. This is a kid who is struggling. Without being intrusive, offer the kind of help that makes this child feel safe with you and supported by you. Start by gently asking some version of, "What can I do for you?"

• DO be yourself. If you like to skydive on weekends, then do it. If you enjoy singing in an 80's-style heavy metal band, then do it. As a parent or stepparent, your authenticity, risk-taking, love of learning, or need for complete silence for an hour a day are part of you—part of what you bring to your partner and your children and stepchildren.

○ DON'T lose yourself when you become a stepparent. Those kids depend on, and learn from, your authenticity.

• DO cocreate the two Bs with your partner: belonging and belief. Every member of your household needs to feel like part of a family—someone who belongs, and is loved, appreciated, and cherished. Everyone also has to believe that you are in this adventure of blending together. That belief is rooted in trust, which can take time to build and always takes intention to build.

○ DON'T put yourself on a short timeline in trying to cocreate the two Bs. You are working on your partnership at the same time you are raising children, so consider this a steady process that can take years.

• DO create a safe haven in your home. Each person must feel emotionally safe to express emotions and be honest.

○ DON'T undermine that by saying things or taking actions that create an "us versus them" feeling between a biological child and a stepsibling.

• DO have a parental outline of acceptable behaviors and unacceptable behaviors. Include age-appropriate rewards and punishments in that outline so there are no surprises for you, your partner, and your children. One example was mentioned in the story of how structure helped a family of eight kids to blend. Mom and dad had a standing rule that beds were made before breakfast was served. A violation cost $10.

○ DON'T be inconsistent about these behaviors and their consequences. In the family of eight, a violation wasn't $10 one day, no dessert the next, and getting grounded another day. Consistency supported success with the household policy.

• DO have a family mission statement. We suggest something like this: "We strive to have every member of our family feel supported and thrive."

NOTES

1. Nicholas H. Wolfinger, *Understanding the Divorce Cycle: The Children of Divorce in their Own Marriages*, Cambridge University Press, 2005.

2. Ibid., p. 113.

3. Ibid., p. 74.

4. John Mordechai Gottman and Robert Wayne Levenson, "The Timing of Divorce: Predicting When a Couple Will Divorce Over a 14-Year Period," *Journal of Marriage and the Family* 62 (August 2000): 737–745; http://ift-malta.com/wp-content/uploads/2013/01/gottman-predictor-of-divorce.pdf

5. The Gottman Institute Blog (Ellie Lisitsa, staff writer), "The Four Horsemen: Introduction," April 22, 2013; http://www.gottmanblog.com/four-horsemen/2014/10/29/the-four-horsemen-introduction.

6. Anderson Cooper as captured in a video on a Gottman Institute website; http://www.gottmanblog.com/four-horsemen/2014/10/30/the-four-horsemen-contempt?rq=four%20horsemen.

7. Trevor Crow and Maryann Karinch, Forging Healthy Connections, New Horizon Press, 2013, p. 45.

8. The Gottman Institute Blog (Ellie Lisitsa, staff writer), "The Four Horsemen: Stonewalling," May 20, 2013; http://www.gottmanblog.com/four-horsemen/2014/10/30/thc-four-horscmcn-stoncwalling?rq=four%20horsemen.

9. Suze Orman, "A Couple's Guide to Managing Money," Yahoo! Finance; http://biz.yahoo.com/pfg/e39couple/

10. Suze Orman, "Your Money Vows," Yahoo! Finance; http://biz.yahoo.com/pfg/e39couple/art011.html.

11. Roger Fisher and Daniel Shapiro, as cited on the Gottman Blog, July 3, 2013; http://www.gottmanblog.com/archives/2014/10/30/finding-common-ground-the-harvard-negotiation-project?rq=collaboration.

Index